PETER AND THE CHURCH

ABOUT THE BOOK

Otto Karrer, who has devoted much of his work to study-
ing and promoting Christian unity, examines Oscar Cullmann's challenging theses concerning the primacy of Peter
in the Church. The prominent Protestant theologian went
further than others before him in recognizing the Catholic
character of the early apostolic Church, but he retained the
traditional Protestant view that Peter was only the primus
of the early Church. Disputes over the position of the Roman Pontiff in the Church have traditionally centered upon
the so-called primacy texts, especially Matthew 16:18
("Thou art Peter . . ."). Cullmann in his *Peter: Disciple,
Apostle, Martyr* contended that no conclusions can be derived from that primacy concerning the apostolic succession
and indeed the papacy as it developed. For him it is clear
that Peter at an early date yielded his primacy to James the
Less (whose position in the early Church has long intrigued
scholars), and that the Catholic case for the apostolic succession
is inadequately founded in the Scriptures. Cullmann's book
was something of a landmark in theological controversy;
it was free from any spirit of hostile polemic against the
Catholic Church or the Papacy. The author hoped for some
frank response from the Catholic side and it is here given
by Father Karrer.

QUAESTIONES DISPUTATAE

OTTO KARRER

PETER
AND THE CHURCH

AN EXAMINATION
OF CULLMANN'S THESIS

06291

HERDER AND HERDER

1963

HERDER AND HERDER NEW YORK

232 Madison Ave., New York 16, N. Y.

Original edition
"Um die Einheit der Christen, 3. Teil"
Verlag Josef Knecht, Frankfurt am Main.
Translated by Ronald Walls

Nihil Obstat: Joannes M. T. Barton, S. T. D., L. S. S.
Censor deputatus

Imprimatur: † Georgius L. Craven, Epus. Sebastopolis, Vic. Cap.
Westmonasterii, die 7ᵃ Feb., 1963.

The Nihil Obstat and Imprimatur are a declaration that a book or pamphlet
is considered to be free from doctrinal or moral error.
It is not implied that those who have granted the Nihil Obstat and Imprimatur
agree with the contents, opinions or statements expressed.

Library of Congress Catalog Card Number: 63-10690

First published in West Germany © 1963 Herder KG

Printed in West Germany by Herder

CONTENTS

CONTENTS

I

PETER AND THE CHURCH

CULLMANN's *Peter* reveals an unusual understanding of the Catholic mind. The author does not confront Catholics with "conditions" upon which he is willing to discuss with them. We experience Christianity in different traditions, denominations, theological systems; but we are conscious of what we have in common in Christ. We are able to talk with one another, and we must talk, for Christ's sake. Cullmann seeks to engage in such a conversation and in writing his book, *Peter,* requests that we express our views in response.

Let us begin with the positive part in which Cullmann makes a solid contribution to ecumenical theology, to the toughest problem in that field – the primacy of Peter. A few supplementary points may serve to consolidate the results.

1. The primacy of Peter

"Thus according to all three Synoptic Gospels Peter indubitably played the rôle of spokesman among the twelve disciples. Furthermore, according to the Gospels of Matthew and Luke,[1]

[1] Matt. 16:17ff.; Luke 22:31f.

Jesus appointed him specially to carry out later the mission of strengthening his brothers."[2] In John 21:15ff.: "On the one side, that position is explicitly recognized, while on the other side, it is reduced by being confronted with the unique position of the Beloved Disciple."[3] It is obvious, however, that the Johannine pastoral symbolism, "feed my lambs, feed my sheep", "includes the two activities ...: leadership of the primitive church in Jerusalem and missionary preaching."[4] "In The book of Acts we clearly note that Peter takes a unique position in the primitive church in Jerusalem."[5] The conversion of the heathen Cornelius, and hence the primary opening of the door of the faith to the heathen through Peter's agency is acknowledged not only by Cullmann, but by modern critical scholarship in general.[6] It is significant for Peter's position in the primitive Christian community, "that Paul, who does not yet know him personally, undertakes the journey (to Jerusalem) only on his account."[7] It is Peter, too, who witnesses the first Easter apparition. "Here

[2] Oskar Cullmann: *Peter* p. 28. All references to this work are to the second revised and expanded English edition, S. C. M. Press, London 1962.
[3] *Ibid.* p. 30.   [4] *Ibid.* p. 65.   [5] *Ibid.* p. 34.
[6] It is true that M. Dibelius (*Theol. Lit.-Ztg.* 1947, 193ff.) and, even more, H. J. Schöps (*Theologie u. Geschichte des Judenchristentums* 1949, 445f.) are inclined to see a tendency in Luke to glorify Peter in the Acts. Cullmann does not define his attitude on this point (*Peter* p. 37f.). It seems hardly credible, however, that Paul's friend and travelling companion would have been specially tempted to exalt Peter above his deserts. He writes in the same "Petrine" way as Matthew does, that is expressing the common mind of the early Church, from whose tradition he drew – setting aside the fact that Matthew might have been included in his literary sources. See J. Schmidt: *Das Ev. nach Lk. (Regensb. Bibel)* 1951, 13.
[7] Gal. 1:18; *Peter* p. 40.

8

at any rate we stand upon solid ground, . . .";[8] and Cullmann knows how to interpret that: by this Easter revelation of the Lord, Peter received a special authority and mission as primate above the others.[9]

Very properly, Cullmann devotes a thorough discussion to the promise of the primacy to Peter as recorded in Matthew 16:17 ff. The careful spade-work which supports his exegesis of the text has been provided by a series of scholars, notably by F. Kattenbusch, S. Euringer, J. Jeremias, K. L. Schmidt, E. Caspar, R. N. Flew, E. Stauffer, A. Oepke.[10] The exceptionally valuable study of J. Jeremias has demonstrated how the rhythm of the Aramaic-Greek verse construction is important in the interpretation of the text. The text runs:

"Blessed art thou, Simon Bar-Jona;
because flesh and blood hath not revealed it to thee,
but my Father who is in heaven.
And I say to thee: Thou art Peter (the rock);
and upon this rock I will build my church;
and the gates of hell shall not prevail against it.
And I will give to thee the keys of the kingdom of heaven,
and whatsoever thou shalt bind upon earth, it shall be
bound also in heaven;
and whatsoever thou shalt loose upon earth, it shall be
loosed also in heaven."

[8] 1 Cor. 15:3 ff.; Luke 24:34; cf. Matt. 16:7. *Peter* p. 59.
[9] E. Stauffer: *Theologie des N. T.* (⁴1948) 17; cf. *Peter* p. 64.
[10] F. Kattenbusch in: *Theol. Stud. u. Krit.* 1922, 96 ff.; S. Euringer in: *Festschr. f. A. Ehrhard* (1922) 141 ff.; J. Jeremias: *Golgotha u. d. hl. Felsen* (1926) *(Angelus II)*; Art. *Kleis* in *Th. Wb.* III, 743 ff.; K. L. Schmidt in: *Th. Bl.* 1927, 293 ff.; Art. *ekklesia* in *Th.Wb.* III, 502 ff.; E. Caspar: *Über die Ursprünge der Primatslehre* (1927; R. N. Flew: *Jesus and his*

The authenticity of this text cannot reasonably be contested; and although there are many shades of opinion amongst modern scholars, all – even the critics – agree in their various fashions with Cullmann: "there is no scientific justification for this denial."[11] It is quite impossible to eliminate this passage from Matthew without doing violence to this Gospel. The passage

Church (²1945) 89ff.; E. Stauffer: *Theol. des N.T.* (⁴1948); A. Oepke: *Das neue Gottesvolk* (1950) 166ff.

[11] *Peter* p. 198 (contradicting Bultmann). The genuineness is disputed by R. Bultmann in: *Th. Bl.* 1941, 265ff.; E. Hirsch: *Frühgesch. d. Ev.* II (1941) 306ff; F. C. Grant: *An Introduction to New Testament Thought* (1950) 270; H. v. Campenhausen: *Kirchl. Amt u. geistl. Vollmacht* (1953) 19, 141. According to Oepke (*op. cit.* 167) their objections amount to this: they have a one-sided conception of "Church" (including ecclesiastical authority) as a juridical institution, and this they attack as an anachronism. Obviously, according to Matthew himself, "The Church had not yet been 'founded' when Jesus uttered these words" (Grant 270), and it is right that H. v. Campenhausen does not wish to put forward an objection (143) based on the juxtaposition of Matt. 16 and Matt. 18, for the supreme authority of one does not abrogate the authority of his co-apostles; but when he says that an "exclusive transfer of the leadership of the whole Church" to the one man Peter "fits neither the evidence of Paul nor the picture given by the Acts" (142), then by "exclusive" he clearly reintroduces the notion that the supreme authority cancels all other authority, whether of the other apostles, of the elders, of the prophets and teachers, and so on. And to say that "as with Matt. 16", so "we can scarcely imagine that" Luke 22:31 ("strengthen thy brethren") and John 21:15ff. ("feed my lambs") "were spoken by Jesus", and that these texts "probably take us beyond the circle of the primitive Church" (19) is to affirm in all sobriety that these New Testament texts are the results of later retrospective projection – more precisely, of falsifications, for in these cases it is inconceivable that there had been any *unconscious* interpolation into the story of the life of Jesus, without appropriate foundation. In this the method of form-criticism seems to overstep the bounds of exegesis.

certainly does not stand in isolation, but is an essential joint in the structure of Matthew, is, in fact, the pivot, the bridge by which the evangelist "connects the historical Jesus with the Church".[12] From the whole mass of the people Jesus had picked out a little band of disciples. These constitute the antithesis to the scribes and the stubborn people. They are the new people of God in embryo, and, after Jesus' return to his heavenly home, are to form the instrument of that reign of God which has come with Jesus. This is what the whole gospel is about – from the first day of his preaching until his death. On the one hand Jesus sought to win over the whole of Israel, on the other hand he concentrated his attention upon his disciples – the remnant of the people. One amongst them is to be the first in this work, one the rock in the might of the "holy mountain" which is Christ. In himself, Peter, who is designated by the revelation of the Father, is a weak man just like the others; but herein is the paradox of divine election: it chooses what is weak. Paul knew this in 1 Cor. 1:27, and to make the fact unmistakably clear, the evangelist immediately goes on to describe the incident which made it plain to Peter and the rest of the disciples.[13]

Cullmann singles out for special attention one objection to the authenticity of the promise to Peter. The report of Peter's Messianic confession in Mark 8:27ff. and in Luke 9:18ff. elicits only the Lord's command to keep silent and then passes on to his prophecies of his Passion. This might very well reflect the original context more accurately – so thinks Cullmann.[14]

[12] *Peter* p. 194; also M.-J. Lagrange: *L'Év. selon St. Matthieu* ([3]1927); K. L. Schmidt in: *Th.Bl.* 1927, 299; J. Schmid: *Das Ev. nach Mt. (Regensb. Bibel)* (1948) 178ff.
[13] Matt. 16:21–3.   [14] *Peter* p. 176ff.

Nonetheless, he by no means wishes to conclude that the text of Matthew is not genuine, that is, does not truly report something which Jesus said. The Lord may have said these things on another occasion, and the evangelist, following his own free grouping of material, have inserted the remarks at this place. The supposed setting of the words is, then, the Last Supper[15], at which, as Luke 22:31 f. reports, a dialogue took place between Jesus and Peter.

"Simon, Simon, behold Satan hath desired to have you, that he may sift you as wheat.

But I have prayed for thee, that thy faith fail not;

and thou, being once converted, confirm thy brethren."

E. Stauffer correctly regards St. Luke's evidence as specially significant for the particular place of Peter.[16] To Peter the Lord entrusted a mediatorial function amongst the brethren, so that he becomes the model of all ministry and service in the Church. The basis and power for this lies in Jesus' high-priestly intercession; and in that, too, the complete confidence of the disciples is founded. All reliance upon human arrogance and boasting are fatuous from the very start, because it is nothing automatic which is given, nothing to be taken for granted: all human authority rests solely upon the power of God's grace, is supported by the intercession of the heavenly high-priest. That is where we look for certainty.

The very same is affirmed by the text about the promise in Matthew. In every line the atmosphere of an Aramaic provenance betrays the primitive origin of this text. There are "not many passages in the Gospels", says Harnack, "through which

[15] *Ibid.* p. 188.   [16] E. Stauffer: *Th. N.T.* [4]16.

12

the Aramaic substratum of thought and form shines so surely as through this clearly defined passage."[17] "Flesh and blood" denotes men as characterized by their natural faculties. "Binding and loosing" is a technical rabbinic expression denoting administration of justice and discipline within the community. Peter is to become "rock", in Aramaic *kepha,* in Greek *petros* – a word expressing sublime concepts and heavy with tradition, as J. Jeremias has shown.[18] Abraham had been the symbol of the holy rock as the "rock of the world";[19] and, according to Daniel 2:34f. and 7:9ff., it is closely associated with the Messianic kingdom which will dash to pieces the kingdoms of the heathen and form a single kingdom out of all nations. The evangelist translates the Aramaic word for rock by the Greek word *petros,* in order to make his readers aware at once of the significance of Peter as the foundation-stone.[20] The whole New Testament makes it quite definite that Simon received the name Peter (rock) from the Lord. "We will find no more convincing ground for this than the confession at Caesarea";[21] and the title "rock" leads to the idea of a building that is to be built in a figurative sense; a self-contained community.[22]

---

[17] A. Harnack: *Berl. S.–Ber.* 1918, 63ff.

[18] J. Jeremias: *Golgotha* (1926) 77.   [19] Strack-Billerbeck: *Kom.* I, 733.

[20] Cf. F. Kattenbusch in: *Festgabe f. K. Müller* (1922) 338.

[21] A. Oepke: *Das neue Gottesvolk* (1950) 167.

[22] Strack-Billerbeck I. 733. According to our Lord's later and undoubtedly genuine saying in John 2:19–22 (Matt. 26:61; Mark 14:58) the new temple of the Messianic holy people will arise by the power of God, while judgment is executed upon the old temple. Clearly this saying is to be taken along with the promise in Matthew 16, and supports it. The Church of the future in place of the old temple fits into Jesus' view of history.

Behind our word "church" is probably the Aramaic *qahal,* the Greek *ekklesia* which means the whole congregation, the people of God. Jesus speaks of "my" church, because to him as the Son of Man "all things have been delegated by the Father"[23]; and now, knowing what his own end is to be, he wants to provide for the future.

There is no reason to assert that the word "church" was unlikely to have been heard from the lips of Jesus. This has been proved by K. L. Schmidt, J. G. H. Hoffmann (Paris) and A. Oepke.[24] Their reasons for believing that Jesus actually had his new community in mind are mainly these: No matter how much we concede to the basic ideas of the methods of form criticism – that the primitive church unconsciously moulded the accounts of Jesus' deeds and sayings, motivated by reverent love –, to mould accounts does not mean to invent their substance. Jesus certainly preached the kingdom of God which was to be realized in him, with the demand that men make their choice. The very first announcement of his message in Mark 1:15 is full of meaning: "The time is accomplished and the kingdom of God is at hand." The whole story of Jesus is full of typological allusions to the Old Testament. That these were all introduced for the first time by the Church without any historical foundation in Jesus' awareness of himself as the fulfilment of the Messianic hope, is an arbitrary assumption which plainly violates the historical understanding of Jesus.[25] He gathered the

---

[23] Matt. 11:27.
[24] K. L. Schmidt in: *Festgabe f. Deissmann* (1927) 259; J. G. H. Hoffmann in: *Mélanges off. à M. Goguel* (1950) 103ff; A. Oepke: *Das neue Gottes-volk* (1950) 155; cf. also W. Eltester in: *Zts. nt. W.* 1950–1, 275ff.
[25] A. Oepke: *op. cit.* 155.

twelve apostles and the seventy disciples as the counterpart to the representatives of the people of the old Covenant,[26] and affirmed his Messiah-ship in fulfilment of the ancient promise, although not in the style of popular contemporary expectation, by assuming the title "Son of Man" and finally by his royal entry into Jerusalem and the declaration before his judges. The Messiah, however, has his Messianic people. The old people of God is to be renewed, "sublimated" (W. Eltester), and finally, with Israel's blindness, superseded by the new people of faith. And so there are the cleansing of the temple to the accompaniment of the saying about re-building,[27] the judgment-discourse about the kingdom passing to others,[28] and the new name for Peter as the "rock" of the new building, of which Jesus himself is the "cornerstone".[29]

When W. G. Kümmel,[30] therefore, tries to prove that the phrase "my church" was first coined in the early days of the apostolic tradition and passed from there – not from Jesus himself – into the gospels, Cullmann is right to see something inconclusive and self-contradictory[31] in his reasoning. There can be no doubt that Jesus as the Son of Man desires to gather together the "saints of the most High" of Daniel 7:25, that is the people of the Covenant whom the Father has given him,[32]

[26] See especially Matt. 19:28.   [27] See above, note 22.
[28] Matt. 8:11f.; 22:8f.; 23:38f.   [29] Mark 12:10.
[30] W. G. Kümmel: *Kirchenbegriff u. Geschichtsbewußtsein in der Urgemeinde und bei Jesus* (1943) 39ff.
[31] *Peter* p. 201 n. 34.
[32] Cf. F. Kattenbusch: *op. cit.* 332; K. L. Schmidt: *op. cit.* 258ff. The references in his *Eschatologie d. Evv.* (*Th. Bl.* 1936, 233) show how close Kümmel's denial approaches an affirmation. According to Luke 10:18 and Mark 13:16 the kingdom of God has already begun. It has appeared

so that the matter which the phrase "my church" denotes certainly goes back to Jesus himself. In his disciples he formed for himself the germ of the Messianic community of salvation for whom the Kingdom is destined.[33] Jesus' institution of the church does not, therefore, stand or fall with this passage in St. Matthew, for it is not an isolated act recorded only in this place, but arises from Jesus' action upon and total attitude towards his people, out of whom he gathered together a group of disciples whom he trained to be a community of witnesses to the kingdom of God. "And so, the question: did Jesus form his disciples into a church? must be answered in the affirmative."[34]

"The gates of Hades shall not prevail against it." Again this links up with ancient Jewish ways of thinking. "Hades" is the expression for the kingdom of the dead, in this context, the kingdom of evil, demonic powers. Whether the correct translation is: they will "not prevail" against the Church, or they will "not overcome" the Church, can be left an open question[35], for however we translate, the demonic powers have no prospect of success in the final battle. The weight, however, seems to lean towards the customary translation: the hostile underworld will wage war on the kingdom of God but will not prevail

with Jesus, and his disciples are "not, indeed, the start of a new community" (which is already there), but chosen "ambassadors of the message of the kingdom". Jesus had in mind, then, a community of future members of the kingdom of God which was already at work in the present and was realized in Jesus. All things revolved round him, the presence of the Messiah-King who "does not wish to unveil apocalyptic events", but "in view of the demands of God revealed in Christ, calls to obedience".

[33] Luke 12:32.   [34] K. L. Schmidt: *op. cit.* 292.   [35] *Peter* p. 208.

against it. R. Bultmann, too, has referred to the eschatological perspective of this passage;[36] and J. Jeremias clearly explains why it cannot be the world of the dead in general, the "power of death" which is the theme. In Jesus' eschatological view, as in that of his Jewish contemporaries, the future life of the faithful departed has nothing whatever to do with the underworld. "The dead who are Christ's have already been awakened to life at the start of the millennium.[37] They no longer belong to the underworld."[38]

The question may be asked: is it against Peter, or the Church, that the powers of evil will be powerless? Jeremias takes the pronoun to apply to Peter because it is he who has been addressed in every line: A. Oepke[39] thinks it correct to make the traditional translation apply to the Church. But because Peter and the Church belong together in any case, the difference in thought is of little consequence.

Jeremias has proved so convincingly that it is Peter himself who is described as the rock of the Church, and neither "the faith he has professed", as Ambrose, Augustine, Chrysostom, Hilary and Leo I thought,[40] nor "Christ himself and alone",

---

[36] R. Bultmann in: *Zts. nt. W.* 1919–20, 165 ff. – although the tense "I shall build" – better, "I desire to build" only emerges in Semitic language from the context. See J. Horst in: *Zts. nt. W.* 1943, 141.

[37] Detailed references for contemporary expectation are given by H. Zeller in: *Zts. f. kath. Theol.* 1949, 392 ff.

[38] J. Jeremias: *Golgotha (Angelus II)* 109.

[39] A. Oepke: *op. cit.*

[40] These authorities were cited in the Reformation period – by, for example, the Schmalkald articles 28 f. (J. Müller: *Die symbolischen Bücher* 1907, 334). Obviously, however, in their interpretations the fathers had no intention of raising the question of Peter's pre-eminence, much

as Luther thought,[41] that nowadays no scientific exegete is likely to repeat these earlier interpretations. "The rock can only mean Peter the man."[42] "The context of the verse shows that 'upon this rock' can be made to apply to nothing except to Cephas."[43] It is true that Christ himself in a pre-eminent sense is "the rock", or "the holy mountain" of Isaias 28:14ff., the "foundation" of 1 Cor. 3:11; but what he has received from the Father, he delegates to his designated representative during the time when he himself will be with the Father.

That such delegation is possible need not be discussed. Just as God or Christ is "shepherd" in the original sense,[44] but there are other "shepherds" who tend Christ's flock in a derivative sense,[45] so it is with the rock. For that matter, in Jewish tradition Abraham and Moses are called "the rock which God used as a foundation upon which to build the world".[46]

With reference to the "keys of the kingdom of heaven", that is of the kingdom of God, which Jesus wishes to give to Peter, Cullmann finds the traditional interpretation of the Church substantiated: Christ is the master of the house who possesses the key,[47] and he hands over to Peter his steward the

less of stressing the reason which was decisive for the transmission of the primacy. Thus M. Meinertz: *Theologie des N.T.* I (1950) 74, is following the fathers and not making "a concession to the Protestant interpretation" as Cullmann thinks – *Peter* p. 213.

[41] Sermon on Peter and Paul 1522, Weimar edition 40 I, 68.

[42] Ed. Schweizer: *Gemeinde nach dem N.T.* (1949) 12.

[43] W. G. Kümmel: *Kirchenbegriff* (1943) 57.

[44] Ps. 22:1; Ezech. 34:23; John 11:14.

[45] Jer. 3:25; John 21:15; Eph. 4:25; 1 Pet. 5:2.

[46] J. Jeremias: *Golgotha (Angelus II* 1926).

[47] Isa. 22:22; Apoc. 1:18.

key, that is supreme authority to open the door to those who desire to belong to the people of God, and to guard the house against its enemies.

With Cullmann[48] we think obviously first and foremost of normative Christian preaching – I add the adjective "normative" in Cullmann's own sense; for the very reason that the strong bunch of keys is given to one man, "an Oriental symbol of authority and ruling in general."[49] As master of the Messianic community of redemption, Christ delegates the keys of the royal kingdom of God, that is the authority of spiritual leadership of the community, to Peter.[50]

"Bind-loose" elucidates what is said about the keys, and like everything else in this passage about the promise, applies to the future for which the Lord wishes to provide in advance. Aramaic usage determines the symbolism of the phrase "bind and loose". This denotes permitting – prohibiting: excommunicating – absolving.[51] With Cullmann we are able to think primarily of that "forgiving" and "retaining" of which the Lord speaks in John 20:23, without excluding responsibility for teaching and discipline for which there is contemporary evidence.

In "binding and loosing" both in Matt. 16:19 and 18:18 H. v. Campenhausen[52] sees primarily an expression of the power to forgive sins, but thinks, however, that this can scarcely be a genuine saying of Jesus, "because the saying must in any case presuppose an existing, defined community". 1. Obviously

---

[48] *Peter* p. 210.
[49] H. v. Campenhausen: *Die Schlüsselgewalt der Kirche* 1937.
[50] *Th.Wb.* II, 750. [51] Strack-Billerbeck I, 738.
[52] H. v. Campenhausen: *Kirchliches Amt u. geistliche Vollmacht* (1953) 137.

an existing community is not presupposed, but the thought and conviction is present that it will come into being. 2. That Jesus had the community in mind has already been proved. 3. An analogous and certainly genuine parallel saying about "binding and loosing" is to be found in Matt. 19:28 where we are told that the Twelve will "judge the tribes of Israel". The symbolism of the words is plain: a new people of God, corresponding to the twelve tribes of Israel, will arise, and the Twelve are its representatives. This new people of God is conceived as belonging to the future, for it first appears after the rejection of the Messiah.[53] As a result, von Campenhausen's discussion on the presumed *Sitz im Leben,* which may account for the origin of the testimony in Matthew 16, becomes unnecessary. Was it Rome? An "arbitrary" assumption of Bonaiuti. Jerusalem? Unlikely. Antioch? Probable.[54] How incredible that the other Christian communities should have accepted this Trojan horse from Antioch if they had not known about the primacy of Peter from the Lord himself! And there is more yet to consider: the Petrine hydra has several heads. If we strike off the one in Matthew 16 others sprout from Luke 22:31f. and John 21:15ff. Which were the communities who bred these primacy-texts from within themselves? Form-criticism becomes tangled in far too many difficulties by trying to doubt that the Lord himself delegated the first spiritual authority to Peter.

It is true that the other apostles are to "bind and loose"[55] – but Peter is to take the lead in this, is to exercise the function

---

[53] Cf. A. Oepke: *Das neue Gottesvolk* (1950) 168.
[54] H. v. Campenhausen: *op. cit.* 142f.
[55] Matt. 18:18.

"in a special way" as Cullmann puts it.[56] He carries the bunch of keys of spiritual authority which is more exactly described as "binding and loosing". In their own time the Twelve as a body will be given authority corresponding to their first mission in Matthew 10:3. They are ambassadors of the kingdom of God which has already appeared with Jesus, as Luke 12:32 proclaims. In this connection we may refer to Cullmann's relevant arguments against a misunderstanding of Jesus' expectation of the end of the world, in which he demonstrates that Jesus expected an indeterminate period of time to follow his death.[57]

Or is it that in Matthew 18:18 the "community" is being addressed? This is E. Schweizer's view[58] and his reasoning resembles that of E. Brunner and H. v. Campenhausen. The primitive community may well have laid more store by a regulated order than did the Pauline Church. Paul knows of no presbyters in his congregations.[59] But this order "in no way" confers certain functions such as the "binding" or "loosing" upon special officials to the exclusion of the rest of the faithful. This accords with the fact that the Acts of the Apostles presupposes that anyone is able to baptize and "even to break bread as well" – although admittedly the latter is "less clear". Against this we find in the Biblical sources that the apostolic holders of office, according to the importance of any question arising, do indeed hear what the congregation has to say, but they them-

---

[56] *Peter* p. 212.
[57] *Ibid.* p. 199; p. 206.
[58] Ed. Schweizer: *Gemeinde im N.T.* (1949) 18.
[59] One might compare with this, Acts 14:22; 20:17ff.; Phil. 1:1; Heb. 13:17 – Pauline congregations.

selves take the lead and make the decision;[60] and according to Titus 3:10 it is "not the congregation, but the authorized representatives of the apostles who settle the matter".[61]

2. *The problem of apostolic succession*

The problem of apostolic succession, and especially of succession of Peter is indeed the crux in the discussions between Catholic and Protestant theologians and it is the hardest problem. As has been observed with reference to the hierarchy, we are concerned not only with a purely theological question, but also with psychological and historical factors which in practice are extremely powerful in their effects. In the sixteenth century the initial theological dispute turned into a schism in the Church when, through political forces, mutually exclusive organizational forms evolved and then received theological support. Conversely, agreement upon this chief problem might indeed end the division of the churches theoretically, and what remained would not necessarily be divided. But even supposing that the theological discussions could solve the question of succession in its two aspects – the episcopal and the Petrine – although the spiritual results would certainly not be inconsiderable, nonetheless for the re-union of the separated confessions, most important spiritual and practical pre-conditions would still be lacking. It is sheer intellectualism to imagine that the ecumenical problem is a purely theological question. What could be envisaged for spiritually-minded men as individuals

[60] See note on Acts 6:6 in Karrer's edition of N.T.
[61] *Th.Wb.* I, 743 ff.

cannot be simply transferred to the collective entities behind them. The Christian communities possess not only their various mental habits, but to a certain extent also their different forms of life, different traditions, systems of education, and a host of imponderable sentiments acquired in the course of many generations. For this very reason the spiritual leaders and pastors of congregations have a responsibility which cannot be solved in purely individualistic terms. We know this in our hearts even if our consciousness is not aware of it. And so, although the theological discussion of this problem may be carried on under the brightest light of the intellect, for men who think realistically, the psychological mechanism of the individual unconscious mind and the secret influences of collective soul cannot be left out of account. So much then by way of introduction to the following theological discussion of the apostolic succession.

As far as the question of Peter's relation to his fellow apostles and to the primitive church is concerned, Cullmann's view coincides with the Catholic interpretation of Scripture. This is all the more significant as Cullmann may be regarded as the representative of many, even if a left wing seeks to assert itself theologically on the question of Church order as on other questions. It would be an illusion to think, however, that Cullmann has thus already built a bridge to unity in terms of the doctrine of the primacy of Peter. The basis of unity is broader in his case than in the case of Emil Brunner, in as much as Cullmann recognizes the Catholic character of the primitive apostolic church. For him it was a hierarchically guided community of faith and love founded by Jesus. For the unity of the post-apostolic church a theme is thus brought to mind which formerly, so it seems to us, Protestantism in its fear of Catholic elements would not admit at all, or only with the most cautious provisos. In essentials, however, that is to say on the question of the succession of Peter and the apostolic succession in general, Cullmann still follows the traditional Protestant line; and he supports his position with reasons which are not so easily disposed of as are many others. This is precisely because he is deaf to the main arguments commonly used in support of the Petrine office. According to him Peter was the primus of the apostolic community, but, in Cullmann's view, no conclusion about the papacy follows from that fact.

First of all we will set out his fundamental ideas and their supporting arguments, then we shall proceed to examine them. His basic argument is as follows.

Peter was primus only during the period of the first beginnings of the Church. After about a decade James took over his position as leader of the primitive church, and Peter gave his whole mind to missionary work. When Peter died in Rome there was therefore no presupposition that he was to have a successor in the primacy, and the connection of the primacy with a particular congregation such as Rome is without foundation.

The succession in the apostolic office is not of decisive importance for the unity of the Church. It may be useful, one possible form among divers others, but certainly not the sole legitimate form of vocation to ministry within the Church.

The unity of the post-apostolic church rests essentially upon the Word of God in Holy Scripture.

All of this Cullmann presents, not in a spirit of hostile polemic against the Catholic Church or the papacy, but for theological and historical reasons, to which he attributes, if not universal, complete certainty, at least sufficient reliability to allow him on the one hand to believe his Protestant viewpoint to be honestly founded, and on the other to hope for some advance from the side of Catholic expression of opinion in the direction of Christian truth and love.

II

THE CULLMANN THESIS

*1. Peter was primus only during the early days,
and was succeeded by James*

a. Biblical proof:

THE Acts of the Apostles 12:17 evidently marks a phase in the activity of Peter and also in his position in the primitive community.[1] According to this information, "Peter departed to another place". It would be wrong to suppose that with the flight of Peter, Jerusalem ceased to hold pride of place.[2] There can be no hint of a "transposition" of the seat of primacy to Antioch or Rome "as E. Stauffer suggests"[3] and Catholic theology asserts.[4] Apparently a sharing out of functions between James and Peter had gradually developed; at any rate, as the fleeing Peter left behind the instructions: "tell these things to James and to the brethren,"[5] that would mean that James

---

[1] *Peter* p. 39. This sentence on p. 37 of the German edition should have been more correctly translated in the sense here given.

[2] *Ibid.* p. 36 note 9.

[3] *Theologie d. N.T.* ([4]1948) 32.

[4] Cullmann is thinking specially of P. Gaechter in *Zts. f. kath. Theol.* 1948 1 ff.; and R. Graber: *Petrus der Fels* (1949).

[5] Acts 12:17.

"became, as it were, his deputy", indeed, it would indicate "the final transfer of the leadership to James".[6]

By the time of the Apostolic Council the transference of the leadership of the community to James the Lord's brother must have been an accomplished fact, for "Already in this connection Paul indirectly asscribes[7] to him the presiding rôle among the 'pillars'." The sequence: James – Cephas – John is certainly no accident.[8]

In his mission within the Jewish Christian sector Peter was obviously dependent upon Jerusalem – and upon James: only so can we explain why Peter, according to Galatians 2:12 feared James' party and had to "dissemble" because of them.[9]

James' presidency over the council appears from the fact that he "draws the conclusion from what has been heard and also formulates the 'decree'."[10]

According to Cullmann, the dispute between Peter and Paul at Antioch proves that "from the time when each begins to exercise his parallel mission, no one can speak of a 'primacy' of Peter in relation to Paul".[11]

b. Post-apostolic evidence

That the transference of leadership from Peter to James affected the leadership of the whole community is made clear by the following facts – so Cullmann thinks in spite of the contrary judgment of other Protestant scholars like E. Fascher.[12]

---

[6] *Peter* p. 42. The German original has: "sozusagen sein Stellvertreter wurde" which Cullman's translator falsely rendered by "must already have taken his place".   [7] Gal. 2:1 ff.   [8] *Peter* p. 43.
[9] *Ibid.* p. 44.   [10] *Ibid.* p. 51.   [11] *Ibid.* p. 49.
[12] E. Fascher in: *Pauly-Wissowa*, 1342, quoted by Cullmann p. 44 note 33.

The Pseudo-Clementine writings. According to these, every teacher in the Church had to be accredited by James. Peter set out to oppose Simon the sorcerer on James' instructions.[13] Peter was required to give account of himself "to James, bishop of the holy Church", and sent him his doctrinal lectures. Clement calls him "bishop of the bishops", "leader of the holy church of the Hebrews and of the churches founded everywhere by God's providence".[14]

Hegesippus – in Eusebius II, 23, 14. According to Hegesippus, "The brother of the Lord, James, takes over the leadership of the Church 'with the apostles' or 'from the apostles'."[15] In addition there is Clement of Alexandria, in Eusebius II, 1, 3, according to whom after the Ascension Peter, James the son of Zebedee and John renounced their pre-eminence and elected James the Just, bishop of Jerusalem. This, however, is the mistaken pre-dating of a later stage back into the early period. Otherwise the Alexandrian Clement stresses Peter's special position.[16]

2. The Catholic idea of apostolic succession is not adequately supported

Peter shares the apostolic dignity with others who are, as the Apocalypse 21:14 says, foundations in the wall of the holy city.[17] But the apostolic dignity is unique and non-recurrent. The apostles did indeed hand on to the elders (bishops) "the

[13] *Peter* p. 41 note 25.   [14] *Ibid.* p. 230.
[15] *Ibid.* p. 229 – but translated by R. W.
[16] *Ibid.* p. 230 note 25.   [17] *Ibid.* p. 222.

leadership, but not their own apostolic office".[18] "The functions of leading and doing missionary work do indeed continue", but not that of the apostle.[19] The direct commission of the first eye-witnesses by the Lord gives the apostolic office a unique quality. As Cullmann knows, that is the teaching of Catholic theology as well. "Therefore they did not install any 'apostles' as successors in leadership, but rather 'bishops' and 'elders'. In what way the latter in turn are to follow one another, the New Testament does not say at all . . ."[20] In his sacerdotal prayer, Jesus prays for the apostles and all who "believe through their word".[21] "Thus the apostles are followed by the entire church of believers. Accordingly the Church has the power of control over the episcopal office, and it is to exercise it as the Holy Spirit guides it."[22]

As an apostle or in connection with the apostolic function, Peter received the primacy amongst the Twelve in the task of laying the foundation of the edifice of the Church;[23] but the testimony of the Gospels and the Acts portrays his special position as something wholly personal and unique. Catholic exegesis proceeds in an arbitrary way "when it tries to find in this text a reference to 'successors'".[24] "On exegetical grounds it must be said that we have no right to see successors addressed in Peter."[25]

In time, Peter's authority is "certainly limited by his martyrdom".[26] "It is only the work of building which belongs to an unlimited future, not the laying of the foundation of the rock on which it is built!"[27] If, in his discourse about building, Jesus has in mind also the post-Petrine period, that only means that the

---

[18] *Ibid.* p. 224.   [19] *Ibid.* p. 220f.   [20] *Ibid.* p. 224.   [21] John 17:20.
[22] *Peter* p. 225; Acts 20:28.   [23] *Peter* p. 221f.   [24] *Ibid.* p. 213.
[25] *Ibid.* p. 215.   [26] *Ibid.* p. 65f.; p. 214.   [27] *Ibid.* p. 214.

commission to be the rock – a once-for-all phase in the history of redemption – is so devised that its effect continues in a unique way after Peter's death.

"And if . . ., Jesus really includes also the period after Peter, . . . this would mean only that the unique mission as rock which the historical Peter fulfils in the redemptive history is of such a character that its unique effectiveness continues even beyond his death . . ."[28]. "We have seen that there must be leadership in the Church, even after the apostolic period when the foundation is laid and down to the present day. In this respect the leadership of the first head of the Church may be example and pattern, but nothing more than this. The leader or leaders of the future Church are given an example in the leadership that is committed to Peter. But Peter himself cannot so to speak arise in every new generation . . . .

"It is a fact that in the beginning a single person stood at the head of the Church as a 'rock' among the 'pillars'. But it is not necessary to conclude from this that also in later times a single person must stand at the head of the entire Church. The entire Church is no longer identical, as it was in the first days, with one local church."[29]

Concerning the location of leadership in the Church, according to Cullmann there is no question of a "translation" of the primacy as a result of Peter's move to Antioch or Rome, because James superseded Peter: Jerusalem continued to be the seat of primacy.[30] The Catholic view links the succession to Peter with a particular congregation, that of Rome, where Peter finally is said to have taken up residence. "But which bishop after him is

[28] *Ibid.* p. 215.   [29] *Ibid.* p. 231.   [30] *Ibid.* p. 229 f.

to play the leading rôle in each case cannot be decided by the principle of a succession. There is no succession in leadership of the entire Church that leads from Jerusalem to another city. This must be stated as a basic proposition."[31] "There is no chain of succession of leaders of the Church at large, . . . In the period after James there is a great gap. In the hortatory writing of Clement which is called the First Epistle of Clement, a bishop speaks in a brotherly way to a sister church, just as also happened elsewhere without any conclusion being drawn that such an act justifies a claim to primacy."[32]

Thus the Church rests "once for all and in every generation upon the foundation that was laid once; . . . How can the Church today still be founded upon the historical person of the apostle Peter?

"This is only possible if this very temporal uniqueness of the foundation formed by the apostles is respected, that is, if the historically unique effect of their person and their work continues to exist in our present as a concrete gift from the time of revelation. This unique gift ... is the apostolic Scripture .... In the only New Testament text that explicitly speaks of the relation of the apostles to the Church that follows them -- I refer to . . . John 17:20 – the further working of the apostles is connected not with the succession principle but rather with the word of the apostles: 'those who believe through their word'."[33]

I have reproduced Cullmann's view as faithfully as possible. Now we must examine that view. We will deal with the question about James first and then get down to the biblical foundation for the Petrine and apostolic succession.

[31] *Ibid.* p. 235; p. 234.   [32] *Ibid.* p. 239.   [33] *Ibid.* p. 225 f.

III

CRITICAL APPRAISAL

1. *Was Peter replaced in the leadership by James after a few years?*

CULLMANN is not the first to hold this view. He himself refers to a few of his precursors such as Ed. Meyer,[1] K. Holl,[2] W. Grundmann,[3] H. Strathmann[4] and E. Lohmeyer;[5] but Cullmann has produced the most thorough integration of arguments from Scripture with those based on early Christian evidence.

First of all, it seems to us that if Cullmann's view is correct and his proofs completely sound, not only is the principle of succession unharmed, but on the contrary is confirmed. According to Cullmann and the other theologians just mentioned, James, the brother of the Lord, was not one of the college of twelve apostles but became attached to them only after Easter. Hence Peter had a successor in the primacy – James. The person of the

---

[1] Ed. Meyer: *Ursprung und Anfänge des Christentums* III (1923) 225 f.
[2] K. Holl: *Der Kirchenbegriff des Paulus in s. Verhältnis z. Urgemeinde: Ges. Aufs.* II (1928) 49.
[3] W. Grundmann in: *Zts. f. nt. W.* 1941, 121.
[4] H. Strathmann in: *Zts. f. syst. Theol.* 1943, 239.
[5] E. Lohmeyer: *Gottesknecht und Davidssohn* (1945) 153. H. v. Campenhausen, on the other hand, is incorrectly cited in support of this (in *Zts. f. Kirchengeschichte* 1950–1, 137).

primate may change, therefore the primacy can extend in time. A correction of the Catholic view would then affect solely the historical question: who was the first primate after Peter?

It is humanly conceivable that Peter might have resigned the primacy, just as later Celestine V resigned the papacy, in favour of someone else, in order, from a certain time onwards, to devote himself solely to the missions. He might have been led to make this decision by the impression that the personality of James, who was highly respected amongst the Jews, was better adapted than his own to the favourable development of the Church in the historical situation. For such a decision, we might argue, Peter would be answerable to his Lord alone, for the basic structure of the Church would remain unaffected. Against such purely human speculations, however, there are many serious objections. K. H. Rengstorf[6] says of the apostolic office: "The office of apostle is given for life and can be resigned by him who holds it only at death." It seems to me that this cannot be doubted. Faithfulness to the personal commission of the apostle is inseparable from his faithfulness to the Lord. The same can be said of the first apostle, of the apostolic primate. Peter would have been bound to regard it as a betrayal of his commission, as faithlessness to the Lord who had commissioned him, if he had resigned from the responsibility for the Church given to him personally, unless induced to do so by a specific fresh revelation. Celestine is no true parallel because the pope is not directly commissioned by the Lord and may give back the commission to those from whom he received it. To which revelation of the Lord to

[6] K. H. Rengstorf in W. Zoellner–W. Stählin: *Die Kirche Jesu Christi und das Wort Gottes* (1937) 191.

Peter may we appeal? Is it perhaps to the apocryphal Pseudo-Clementine source which tells us that James was installed as "bishop of Jerusalem" by the Lord himself?[7] Not only does Cullmann himself consider that this information must be used with caution,[8] but it is the product of a Judaistic-Ebionite movement, which comes into the picture again later on. More than that: Cullmann cannot appeal to it in support of a transfer of the primacy from Peter to James, for that apocryphal "episcopal" appointment at the Easter apparition took place at the very first beginning of the Church, and Cullmann requires a "revelation" for his alleged later transfer of the primacy to James.

These things, therefore, do not make Cullmann's opinion about the transfer of primacy to James at all probable.

When he asserts that Peter on his departure – reported in Acts 12:17 – designated James to be primate in place of himself, this is a purely subjective interpretation without objective support from biblical testimony.

No one is asserting that when Peter moved elsewhere Jerusalem lost its status as mother-church and first point of departure of the Christian mission. In Cullmann's phrase, this status is unique, historically inalienable. As Peter stands alone, unique as first amongst the apostles, and as consequently no Pope regards himself in Peter's place as apostle or first apostle in the Church – "the bishops are successors of the apostles, without themselves

---

[7] This statement occurred in the lost "sketches" of Clement of Alexandria, quoted by Eusebius: *H. E.* II, 1. Cf. also Epiphanius: *Haer.* 78, 7; Chrysostom: *In Cor.* h. 38, 4. Undoubtedly their common source is the Ebionite literary foundation of Pseudo-Clement, of which they merely take cognizance without assimilating its historical design.

[8] *Peter* p. 229.

being apostles, let alone the first apostle"[9] –, so Jerusalem is the mother-church once-and-for-all, the starting-point of the Christian mission, and neither Antioch nor Rome could ever lay claim to that name. Even after Peter had departed "to another place", Jerusalem remained the sacred place of origin, the scene of the pentecostal event, and remained so for ever in the mind of Christendom even when this place had become a heap of ruins and not a single Christian lived there any more.

Jerusalem was the mother-church, but that it had any prospect of remaining for long the centre of Christendom, could not be the view of any Christian. Our Lord's prophecy of the judgment of the city and his command in Mark 13:14 to flee from the abomination of desolation is proof enough of that; and, as is well known, the Christians who still lived in Jerusalem did flee into east Jordania at that time. At the time of Peter's flight things had not gone so far. Next to the murder of James the elder in A.D. 42 it was but the second preparatory sign of the approaching catastrophe. For the time being, following the instructions of the departing Peter, the Lord's kinsman, James, stayed behind. The situation quietened down once more – James' prestige certainly had much to do with this – so that in the year 50 Peter was able to put in a passing appearance at the Apostolic Council, as described in Acts 15.

Had the situation in Jerusalem at that time not been perfectly calm, they would undoubtedly have assembled elsewhere – in Caesarea perhaps –, but the memory of Pentecost and the love of the mother-church pointed, whenever possible, to Jerusalem. If Paul even, who was attacked by the Jewish Christians, sought to

[9] G. Söhngen: *Die Einheit in der Theologie* (1952) 307.

keep alive amongst the gentile Christian congregations piety towards the Jewish-Christian mother-congregation, and again later
vigorously took up the cause of resolving the tension between
Jewish and gentile Christianity,[10] how much more must Peter,
who bore prime responsibility for the unity of the Church, have
cherished a love for Jerusalem. But what has all this to do basically with the "primacy of Jerusalem"? If the "word of the Lord
goes forth from Jerusalem"[11] does that mean that the salvation
of the people of God is bound up with the "earthly Jerusalem
below"?[12] Has the Jewish-Samaritan dispute[13] as to whether the
"true worshippers" worship on Gerizim or Sion not long been
obsolete for Christians? We should keep this in mind when we
come later to discuss whether or not Rome will be the "perma-
nent" seat of the Petrine succession.

Whilst Peter was engaged in an early stage of missionary travel
in Joppa and Caesarea, and meanwhile in Jerusalem James
was slowly rising to a position of special prestige in the original
congregation, was Peter "permitted" at that time to regard himself as competent to make such a far-reaching decision as that
about the reception of heathen into the Church without demand-
ing the fulfilment of the Law?[14] Without any doubt he was, –
although whilst he was occupied in apostolic journeys, James was
the "pillar" of the Jerusalem church. And who would attempt to
deduce a "counter-proof" against the validity of the Petrine
office from the circumstance that Peter justified his decision
before the Jewish Christians of Jerusalem?[15] According to Cull-

[10] Acts 21:17–26.   [11] Isa. 2:3.
[12] Cf. Gal. 4:25f.   [13] John 4:2.
[14] Acts 10.   [15] Acts 11:1.

mann himself, he was still chief shepherd[16] at that time, resigning only later on.[17] Because the pastoral office as Jesus meant it, and as Peter, or the early church conceived it is not a lordly dominion, but directs the holder of the office to lead the flock in the spirit of love,[18] with understanding of the congregation and "in harmony with the apostolic college",[19] such a declaration and self-justification is completely in harmony with the notion of the Church – and according to our modern conception too.[20] Neither in the primitive church nor in later times do the pastors of the church find their dignity an obstacle in the way of giving account for their policies – neither the bishops to their clergy nor the *primus* amongst the bishops to his colleagues. The great bishop Cyprian (d. 258) wrote to his clergy to say that he would "give an account"[21] to them of his actions; Pope Pelagius I (d. 561) declared himself ready, in accordance with Peter's admonition, "to answer for myself before all who expect me to give an account";[22] the present pope is certainly not play-acting when he performs the ceremony of "mouth opening" with the new cardinals: they are to advise him openly. When Irenaeus ascribes to the Roman church a "specially effective pre-eminence *(poten-*

---

[16] Officially at least, even if Cullmann (*Peter* 37) surmises that even before this a certain sharing of function with James had gradually emerged. And while on p. 37 he considers "self-justification" compatible with the "first position", yet on p. 229 he takes "giving an account of oneself" to be a sign of subordination to James.

[17] Acts 12:17.   [18] Matt. 20:26ff.; John 21:15; 1 Pet. 5:1–4.

[19] E. Stauffer: *op. cit.* 17.

[20] Vat. Council IV, 4: Denzinger n. 1836. Cf. *Revue des Sc. ph.-th.* 1952, 74 – a paper on G. Dejaifre in *Nouv. Rev. Th.* May 1952.

[21] Cyprian: *Ep.* 14, 1.

[22] Pelagius I: *Ep.* 5: Migne PL 69, 399.

37

tior principalitas)", and regards the agreement of all episcopal sees with Rome as the religious principle of unity,[23] this does not prevent him from telling Pope Victor of his objections to pressure being put on the East concerning the Easter dispute; nor is Eusebius a bad churchman because he applauds him for so doing,[24] just as today theologians are not disparaging the importance of the Petrine primacy when they affirm that "an objective examination of the Vatican Council permits the conclusion that its definition has changed nothing in the organic concept of the Church and particularly of the collegiate structure of the hierarchy in the Church".[25]

Obviously we do not mean to suggest the view that the original mode of operation of the spiritual pastoral office has remained the same throughout the whole history of the Church. There are sound Catholic theologians who warn us against "judging the exercise of the (primitive) primacy by modern standards".[26] Outward forms change; and if according to the idea, according to the essence of the Church, "holy ministry and holy people", "apostles and prophets", "special priesthood and priesthood of all believers" make up the Church only together, then in the course of history the emphasis may be pushed now towards this pole of the Christian world, now towards the other. This is but an expression of the fact that the Church is not merely an idea but has a history in time. The integration of the two quantities however, is for ever essential, and if the primitive church, as described in the Bible, is to be held up as a model for the Church in later centuries, then it cannot possibly seem strange if apostles like Peter and Paul, and their colleagues too, are accountable to

---

[23] Irenaeus: *Adv. Haer.* III, 3, 2.   [24] Eusebius: *H. E.* V, 24, 9f.
[25] See above, note 114.   [26] B. Bartmann: *Dogmatik* II (⁸1932) 169.

the Church;[27] if in the First Epistle of Clement – "after the New Testament the most important document which has come down to us from the earliest period in the Church's history"[28] – the congregation with their bishop, an obvious unit, appear as the common author of the good-news; and if once more Ignatius is so much impressed with the unity he sees between congregation and bishop that he greets the congregation in Rome – with their bishop – as "presidents of love".[29]

What, however, has the place where Peter exercised his pastoral office to do with the Church, the residence or "see" of the chief pastor with his ecclesiastical authority as such? Just as the Lord was "the holy rock", the foundation of the Church in the primary sense of the word whether he happened for the moment to be in Judaea or Galilee or Caesarea Philippi, for he is "the rock not in the physical, geographical sense but in the spiritual sense; and as, according to Paul, the ancient people wandering in the wilderness drank of the spiritual rock that followed them; and the rock was Christ"[30]: so the new people of God is joined with the Lord of the Church through the rock, Peter, without the latter having been geographically fixed, for "the rock is to be understood spiritually", the people of God are pilgrims in this world, and Peter the rock of the Church feels that he and his fellow pilgrims are "pilgrims and strangers".[31] The whole trend of primitive Christian life was incompatible with the notion of fixing the function of leadership in one place, not merely because of the eschatological perspective which quickened the conscious-

---

[27] See W. Mundle: *Das Apostelbild des Apg.* in: *Zts. f. nt. W.* 1928, 41.
[28] A. Harnack: *Das Schreiben der röm. Gemeinde an die Korinthische* 1929, 5.
[29] Ignatius: Romans 1:1.   [30] 1 Cor. 10:4.
[31] 1 Pet. 2:11; cf. Heb. 11:13; Hermas: *Shepherd* 1:6.

ness that all things were heading for dissolution, but also from plain experience in this world. The leaders of the Church at least were hunted about from city to city; but the spiritual rock which shares in the strength of the rock that is Christ and represents him, wherever he happened to be, was "the rock" who accompanied the people of the Lord in the wilderness, and, in reliance upon the Lord's intercession, must "strengthen" his brethren.[32]

This primitive Christian consciousness, this experience of being a "third race" after the Jews and the heathen,[33] of being pilgrims upon the earth – expressed so ecstatically by Paul[34] and more soberly but with the very same spirit of faith by Peter[35] – makes quite impossible any fixation of spiritual authority to one particular place. All the spiritual premises are lacking and there is no historical clue either which would justify us in projecting the profane notion of a local restriction of spiritual authority back into the earliest period. E. Stauffer justly says of Peter's crozier: "As Peter received the power of the keys in Matthew 16:19, so in John 21:15ff. he received, from the hand of the glorified archshepherd, the crozier which he was to carry from henceforth until his own death."[36]

We can deduce something about the probable rôle of James in Jerusalem from the Pauline passages cited by Cullmann. He is one of the "pillars". In the lively argument of the Epistle to the Galatians, St. Paul, so concerned to show that the "pillars" ap-

---

[32] Luke 22:32.

[33] See *Kerygma Petri* in: TU 11, 1 (1893) 21 49f. Cf. A. Harnack: *The Expansion of Christianity* (1904) Book II, chap. 6; K. Prümm: *Christentum als Neuheitserlebnis* (1929).

[34] 2 Cor. 4:7–18. [35] 1 Pet. 1:13.

[36] E. Stauffer: *Theol. N.T.* (⁴1948) 17.

prove his preaching a gospel unencumbered by the Law, knows that the psychological effect will be considerable upon the Judaizing opponents if he singles out from the authorities the one whom his opponents recognize as the authority – James. Paul could make his point in no more convincing way. Hence the sequence: "James, Cephas, John" is "no accident". Cullmann is perfectly right, but for quite other and more obvious reasons than he adduces. If Paul had his wits about him, he could argue, this is the sort of sequence that would suggest itself from psychological considerations, but nothing can be deduced from it concerning any theological order of precedence. And there is biblical corroboration; for even now, at a time when, according to Cullmann, James had long since taken Peter's place, Paul most clearly ascribes the precedence to Peter. According to Cullmann the transfer of office had taken place between the beginning and the middle of the year 40. 1 Corinthians 15:5, however, was written in 57. And what do we read there? The account is composed solemnly "in documentary fashion",[37] passing on a tradition: the Risen Lord "was seen by Cephas; and after that by the eleven. Then was he seen by more than five hundred brethren at once . . . . After that he was seen by James; then by all the apostles. And last of all he was seen also by me, as by one born out of due time." That is, Peter was the first, Paul the last to see the Risen One. It is widely recognized – by Cullmann too[38] –

---

[37] K. Holl: *Ges. Aufsätze* (1928) II, 46.
[38] *Peter* p. 69; p. 221. Cf. E. Stauffer: *op. cit.* 17; E. Hirsch: *Die Auferstehungsgeschichte u. d. christl. Glaube* (1940) 18; W. Grundmann in: *Zts. nt. W.* 1940, 119; A. Fridrichsen (see Cullmann: *Peter* p. 221 note 4); H. v. Campenhausen: *Die Nachfolge des Jakobus,* in: *Zts. f. Kirchengesch.* 1950–1, 136f.

that the Easter apparitions reported here were revelations of calling and commissioning in Paul's estimation. That is why he does not mention the women and that is why "the stress on the first revelation must logically imply a special calling, a special commission. Luke and Matthew set the special commission of Peter in the pre-Easter period, Paul and John speak of the days following Easter; but the meaning of all of these special callings is basically the same: the special responsibility of Peter for the emerging church."[39] Thus it is precisely through Paul – besides the indirect testimony of Luke 24:34 – that we know about the Easter revelation to Peter. He singles out Peter as the first and James comes next at some distance. We note that the account derives "from the tradition which grew up and was formulated in the original Jerusalem community"[40] and that Paul could not and had no desire to pass over in silence the "bishop of the church of the Hebrews"; but Paul clearly says nothing about a primacy of James – and this passage was written not long after the Epistle to the Galatians which is supposed to contain proofs of the primacy of James.

Let us examine this closely. Cullmann asserts[41] that according to Galatians 2:11 ff. Peter must have been dependent on James otherwise in Antioch he would not have had "to fear the 'party of James'" to such an extent as to have to "dissemble on their account". On this issue Peter was definitely on the side of Gentile-Christian freedom from the Law, and at Caesarea had already presided at table with the Gentiles, in defiance of the Jewish law.[42] He had acted in the same way in Antioch too, at

[39] E. Stauffer: *op. cit.* 17.
[40] H. Strathmann in: *Zts. f. syst. Theol.* 1943, 241.
[41] *Peter* p. 44.   [42] Acts 10–11.

first, but found himself in difficulties when the "party of James" appeared. Was that perhaps because at that time he was subject to James? Is this explanation of Cullmann's the most obvious one? To me the exact opposite seems to be the truth. It was he as head of the Church who was primarily responsible for the unity of the Church and had to avoid exacerbating the fanaticism of certain "pharisaical" Jewish-Christians[43] who were "behind James" but with whom he was by no means to be identified – as Acts 15:13 ff. shows. Paul, too, had to learn by experience how dangerous these people could become for his community. Galatians, II Corinthians and even the Epistle to the Philippians 1:15 ff. and 3:2 f. show his concern about the intrigues of the "evil dogs". It would be wrong to think that it is Jews who are meant: it is Jewish-Christians from Jerusalem. "The term 'evil workers', in the gospel (Phil. 3:2) is an exact parallel to the 'deceitful workmen' of 2 Cor. 11:13, and it does not fit the Jews against whom, after all, the Philippians required no warning."[44] It was no wonder, then, that Peter feared the Christian Judaizers. He must have thought that his open association with the Gentile-Christians was going beyond the terms of the Jerusalem agreement and that its consequences "meant nothing less than the sacrifice of Jewish Christianity".[45] It is understandable that on the appearance of the confirmed Judaizers he should have tried to find a way out, as best he could, by withdrawing for the time being from communion with them. He was experiencing the same thing as Paul himself, who let Timothy be circumcised for similar reasons,[46] certainly not at

---

[43] Acts 15:5; 15:13 ff.
[44] A. Ehrhard: *Urkirche u. Frühkatholizismus* (1935) 55.
[45] *Ibid.* 50.   [46] Acts 16:3.

his own wish, and who, confronted by James' party, pretended to be a good orthodox Jewish-Christian. We may well apply his characterization of Peter in Gal. 2:13 to his own accommodation to the people of Jerusalem in Acts 21:26. It was not from inclination that he acted in this way but, "for the sake of peace" like Peter.[47] Do we then have to assume that Paul bowed to the "superior authority" of James? This does not appear from Gal. 2:6–10. Why then judge Peter by a different standard? Why should his caution prove that he bowed to the "superior authority"? It seems to me to suffice to keep in mind the truly difficult situation in which Peter found himself. Because of an even greater responsibility for the unity of the Church he tried as far as possible to avoid an open conflict with the Judaistic party. Besides, even as an apostle, Peter no more than Paul ceased to be human. We may here cite a parallel from church history. In the fourth century out of respect for Byzantium Pope Liberius subscribed to a semi-Arian formula which was later condemned by the council.[48] In the seventh century Pope Honorius experienced a similar misfortune over an ambiguous phrase.[49] Who could derive "evidence" from this that in those days "it was no longer Liberius nor Honorius but the Byzantine Patriarch who exercised authority in the Church"?

---

[47] P. Gaechter in: *Zts. f. kath. Theol.* 1948, 42 ff. seems to me to be right to interpret as he does, in contrast to Cullmann (*Peter* p. 44). Like Paul, Peter had reason to fear the Jews. Cullmann's own arguments (*Peter* pp. 95–115) show that there are indications that Peter was eventually brought to his death on a cross in Rome as the result of their denunciations.

[48] See J. H. Newman: *The Arians* (1919) 464.

[49] See Th. Granderath: *Gesch. d. Vat. Konzils* III (1906) 31 ff.

Why pursue these theological points when there are more obvious explanations?

In connection with this, but applied by Cullmann as a special proof of cessation of the Petrine primacy, is the well-known dispute between Peter and Paul at Antioch. Paul's appearance is taken to prove that "from the time when each begins to exercise his parallel mission, no one can speak of a 'primacy' of Peter in relation to Paul."[50] Here, too, there would seem to be a more obvious explanation. Is Paul talking sense or not when he upbraids Peter with "compelling" the others by his behaviour to act as he does?[51] What he says makes sense only if Peter's attitude was decisive. Otherwise it would be meaningless. Otherwise Paul had better argue with others more guilty – the Jerusalem party! Or did he lack courage to do this? Certainly not, he proved his courage and his love for the cause of the gospel. The explanation of another eminent Protestant theologian seems to me to be excellent: "Paul is able to confront Peter with a touch of irony. Nonetheless to Paul even this Peter ensnared by sin (let us say: 'confused by human weakness') clearly remains the one elevated above and marked out from the crowd. It is not men that matter but the Church."[52] As J. L. Leuba puts it: "We are not dealing with contradictions in doctrine. Peter erred by his inconsistancy for which Paul reproached him – and evidently he allowed himself to be corrected."[53] Perhaps the best comment comes from St. Augustine. He took it as proof "that even those not of equal rank

---

[50] *Peter* p. 49. [51] Gal. 2:14.
[52] K. L. Schmidt in: *Th. Bl.* 1927, 300.
[53] J. L. Leuba: *L'Institution et l'Événement* (1950) 61 ff.

may, in defence of the truth of the gospel, oppose a superior – *salva fraterna caritate* – without damaging fraternal love".[54]

The view that at the Apostolic Council Peter appeared "simply as the representative of the mission"[55] whereas James in contrast plainly assumed the "presidency", corresponds exactly to Cullmann's line of argument. Yet on this very point he seems to speak with hesitation and as from personal impression. In fact, not a few sound Protestant scholars deduce the very opposite from the incident. Thus J. Fr. Kleuker could not but testify to his candid impression, that throughout the Acts of the Apostles Peter appeared "in accordance with the Lord's commission, as the first", and again acted as if he were spokesman – at the Council – in the matter of the binding character of the law.[56] "At the Apostolic Council it seems to be taken for granted that Peter has the last word", writes R. Baumann,[57] and Ed. Schweizer, too, feels that Peter appears "at the Council as the one who calls the tune",[58] just as elsewhere in the Acts he appears as "the undoubted leader of the Church". M. Dibelius[59] and H. J. Schöps[60] believe themselves forced to detect in the Acts of the Apostles Luke's explicit tendency to "elevate" Peter, the tendency which later provoked the Ebionites to strike out against the Catholic Church and to circulate their

---

[54] Augustine: *Epistle to Jerome: Ep.* 82, 21. Cf. St. Thomas Aquinas: Commentary on Gal. 2, III (text quoted in Karrer's edition of N.T. on Gal. 2:14).

[55] *Peter* p. 51.

[56] J. Fr. Kleuker: *Johannes, Petrus und Paulus als Christologen* (1785) 143.

[57] R. Baumann: *Des Petrus Bekenntnis u. Schlüssel* (1950) 106.

[58] Ed. Schweizer: *Gemeinde nach dem N.T.* (1949) 12.

[59] M. Dibelius in: *Theol. Lit.-Ztg.* 1947, 193 ff.

[60] H. J. Schöps: *Theologie u. Gesch. d. Judenchrist.* (1949) 445 ff.

own "Acts of the Apostles" which elevated their "Primate James". More of this later. – What is the answer to be? Certainly as far as biblical sources are concerned, Cullmann can rely on no more than subjective impressions. These, however, are not sufficient.

Moreover, according to the principles of present-day scriptural exegesis we must accept it as certain that in the fifties Peter was regarded as primate of the Church, at a time, that is, when, according to Cullmann, he could not have been it; and that he was so regarded within the authoritative circle of the apostles. According to the generally accepted principles of so-called Form Criticism, the accounts of the evangelists received their stamp from the early community tradition. This was their "place in life". For this reason it must be accepted as obvious that a solemn saying like Jesus' promise to the "rock" and "key-bearer of the Church" in Matthew 16 could only have been handed on and entered into the Gospel within the span of a generation in which "the matter referred to was a reality or regarded as an ideal".[61] Hence in the period when Matthew's Gospel came into circulation, Peter must have been known as the leading man in the Church. The Church could hardly have allowed Matthew's Gospel to appear and be circulated, between 50 and 60, if this Peter was indeed living but was not the man he was supposed to be according to the official document. At least in the regions where Matthew's Gospel was current, Peter must have held the dignity of first apostle.[62]

---

[61] H. Strathmann in: *Zts. f. system. Th.* 1943, 354.
[62] H. Strathmann, to whom I am indebted, holds the view that the separate Gospels were originally the "particular property" of their native district. The home of Matthew's Gospel is said to have been Antioch or Syria, where Peter is supposed to have worked for years as a

Of the post-apostolic witnesses of the alleged replacement of Peter by James, Cullmann singles out the so-called *Pseudo-Clementina,* an edifying novel purporting to have been written by Clement of Rome, but being in fact a disjointed work dating from a much later period – the beginning of the third century. The work has been preserved only in two different, possibly independent recensions from the fourth century, the *Homilies* – edifying lectures – and the *Recognitions* – a novel of recognition.[63] "Clement" describes how as a youth in Rome he heard of the epiphany of the Son of God in Palestine, set off for that country, met Peter and became his disciple and in the end, with Peter's help, found his parents and family once more. Within this framework the narrator has collected a wealth of themes of religious instruction which, judging by the sources he used, are not without danger from the standpoint of orthodoxy, but are furnished with so much Catholic counterbalance that guileless readers might fail to see the poison in the honey. This work was in fact fairly widely circulated in ancient times. After laborious analysis of the sources by several scholars, notably H. Waitz,[64] C. Schmidt,[65] and H. J. Schöps,[66]

---

missionary. Cullmann is correct (*Peter* p. 27 n. 39) to find this apportioning a "somewhat artificial scheme". That is to say, Matthew belonged to other regions as well – it was permissible to spread the truth about Peter as supreme pastor in other places as well without embarrassment to the Church. Wherever a church took Matthew (and the same applies to Luke) as the document of its faith, there Peter, and no other, was recognized as the leader.

[63] *Homilies* and *Recognitions* both in Migne PG I.

[64] H. Waitz: *Die Ps.-Klementinen* in:*TU* 1904.

[65] C. Schmidt: *Studien zu den Ps.-Klementinen* in *TU* 1929.

[66] H. J. Schöps: *Theologie u. Gesch. d. Judenchristentums* (1949).

a number of anti-Christian views emerged. Jesus is the ideal man – nothing more; he is the third manifestation of the "great prophet" after Adam and Moses; on his baptism in the Jordan he was possessed by the Spirit and made the reformer of the Jewish people. Whole sections of the Old Testament are rejected; circumcision and baptism by water are essential for membership in the new Israel, the primate of which, according to these sources, is James whose real opponent is represented as Paul. The world is seen as arranged in opposites: light and darkness; spirit and matter; male and female; truth and lies; good and evil. It is thus obvious that, in spite of the Catholic editing by the author, the *Pseudo-Clementina* aroused the special interest of heretical circles. The *Homilies* were edited about 350 by an Arian, the *Recognitions* about 370 by a Eunomian.[67]

In 1930, Cullmann also published an interesting study of the problem of the *Pseudo-Clementina* from the angle of the history of the sources and the history of ideas.[68] Its hypothesis concerning the source-history is not relevant to our purposes. Concerning the history of the ideas, Cullmann finds that the "gnosis" of the Clementine sources – apart from heretical infusions – is closely related to original Jewish-Christianity and St. John's Gospel.[69] What concerns us most of all now,

---

[67] *Op. cit.* 25 ff.; 38 ff.

[68] O. Cullmann: *Le problème lit. et hist. du Roman Ps.-Clémentin* (1930). Cf. the discussion by H. Waitz in: *Zts. f. Kirchengeschichte* III, 1 (1931) 168 ff.

[69] Cullmann: *Le problème* 252 ff. – in company with R. Bultmann, W. Bauer, and apparently especially H. Waitz in: *Zts. f. Kirchengesch. op. cit.* Valuable elucidation on Christian (that is, Johannine) gnosis is given by: E. Percy: *Untersuchungen über den Ursprung der joh. Theologie* (1939); P. Gaechter: *Summa introd. in N.T.* (1938) 138 ff.; esp. R. Guar-

because the view reappears in his *Peter,* is Cullmann's contention that in the field of church history as well, the Clementine sources yield valuable information about the structure of the Jerusalem church reaching back into the apostolic period.[70] According to this, James had been "the bishop of the holy Church", and was not one of the Twelve but their superior, installed by Christ himself.[71] Admittedly Peter possessed greater moral authority, but was subject to James as the "leader and organizer by whom every teacher and apostle had to be commissioned".[72]

Our astonishment grows when we hear Cullmann affirm that this is in harmony with the New Testament. There too, he asserts, James is "a kind of supreme authority for the apostles themselves". "Peter and Paul depend upon James." At a certain moment, the apostles seem to have set off upon the missions, and on his return Paul is "compelled" to take the Jewish Nazirite vow in order to ingratiate himself with the Jerusalem congregation.[73]

In critical elucidation of this appraisal of the *Pseudo-Clementina* by Cullmann it seems appropriate to review more recent research. H. Waitz who initiated research upon the sources of the *Pseudo-Clementina* considered the writer's Catholic attitude, on account of his sources to be somewhat "unclear".

dini: *Jesus Christus, sein Bild in den Schriften des N.T.* II (1940); W. Grossouw: *De Heilsymbolen van het vierde Evangelie* in: *Theol. Opstellen* (Utrecht 1944) 89 ff. F. C. Grant very aptly sums up his judgment on Johannine gnosis: "The quasi-gnostic milieu of the author, against which he is reacting strongly in favour of historical, traditional, institutional Christianity, has nevertheless coloured his outlook." (*An Introduction* 1950 p. 90) Cf. also the paper by W. Eltester in: *Zts. ntl. Wiss.* 1950–1, 270.

[70] Cullmann: *Le problème* 220 ff.
[71] *Recogn.* 1, 43.   [72] Cullmann: *Le problème*.   [73] Acts 21:22 ff.

Some of his sources were "Judaistic or Gnostic".[74] If James seems repeatedly to be set over Peter, then the author was able to "transcribe this guilelessly"[75] for at the same time he provided a Petrine counterbalance by stressing Peter's precedence with the succession to Clement in the introduction. It is Peter too who "carries out the function of a superior bishop by ordaining bishops and presbyters in the most diverse cities – even in Caesarea near Jerusalem".[76] And if even in the "Letter of Clement to James" (a document composed by the author himself) Clement addresses James as "bishop of bishops", this, according to Waitz, "by no means indicates the actual position and dignity of James, least of all at the time when the Clementine novel was written",[77] that is early in the third century.

C. Schmidt follows essentially upon the same lines.[78] He likewise thinks that the writer was a member of the Church who seems, however, in great contrast to the Epistle of Barnabas, to regard the "Mosaic faith as of equal value as Christianity".[79] His Judaistic-Gnostic sources, however, were rendered innocuous by fusion with Catholic material".[80] Besides the apostles James appears as "Bishop of Jerusalem",[81] even as "Archbishop" of Jerusalem, [82] and is compared to Caiphas the high-priest.[83] All of this is culled straight from Judaistic sources to which the author even adapts himself to the extent that, in the rôle of Clement of Rome, he defers to James as the "bishop of bishops". But, C. Schmidt[84] judges, such eastern formulae should not be pressed too far, for:

[74] H. Waitz: *op. cit.* 54f.   [75] *Ibid.* 68.   [76] *Ibid.*   [77] *Ibid.*
[78] C. Schmidt: *Studien* . . . (1929).   [79] *Ibid.* 251.   [80] *Ibid.* 3.
[81] *Recogn.* 1, 44; 55; 69 etc.   [82] *Ibid.* 1, 73.   [83] *Ibid.* 1, 44; 55.
[84] C. Schmidt: *Studien* . . . (1929) 105–7.

First, James is thus named only in the title. Elsewhere he is simply "Lord James"; and the former address is harmless to readers who are taught that Clement, the writer of the letter, is himself the successor in the seat of Peter, the "canon (that is, the authoritative rule) of the Catholic Church".

Second, there is the verdict of Waitz: ". . . It by no means indicates the actual position and dignity of James or of his successors . . . ."

Third, the title really designates "the universal episcopate of James over the 'Church of the Hebrews' with its seat in Jerusalem" which, according to K. Holl, regarded itself as "a single large community", the first of the Palestinian foundations.[85] In other words the exalted form of address is but the suitable title for him who "stands at the head of the presbytery of Jerusalem, on the one hand their bishop, but on the other archbishop also of all the Jewish-Christian communities led by bishops".[86] To my mind, all this accurately reflects the view of "Clement"; but was it also the view of the sources he used? Clearly not, for he was Catholic in thought, they heretical. Thus it remains an open question whether or not his sources contained worthwhile, credible reminiscences of the historical conditions in the primitive church, including those concerning the subordination of Peter to James. In 1930 Cullmann firmly accepted the view that they did, and he retains this view with equal assurance in *Peter* in 1952, in spite of the fact that meanwhile H. J. Schöps[87] has made this very question of the historical reliability of the Clementine sources a main issue in his work, to which H. v. Cam-

---

[85] K. Holl: *Ges. Aufsätze* II (1928) 61.
[86] C. Schmidt: *Studien* 108 n. 2.
[87] H. J. Schöps: *Theologie u. Gesch. d. Judenchristentums* (1949).

penhausen[88] has added valuable supplements. Cullmann knows of both and quotes them, but, it would seem, with thorough misapprehension; for his references to Schöps and Campenhausen could lead one to think that they shared his theses. In fact it is quite the reverse: they distinguish sharply between the history of James and the tendencious legend; and for them the Clementine sources are, so to speak, the classic second century example of such legends.

According to H. v. Campenhausen, linking up with the Easter revelation to James,[89] the Pseudo-Clementine sources are characteristic of that Judaizing development "which wanted to set James not only above Paul but above Peter and all the rest of the disciples also".[90] What is historically credible about James is in the New Testament: along with the "pillars", Peter and John, he won great prestige in the mother congregation, on account of his Easter calling, his kinship with the Lord, and his personal religious character. He became the representative of their Jewish-Christian section,[91] and after the expulsion of the Hellenistic group[92] and after Peter's departure,[93] the *de facto* leader of the congregation of Jerusalem.[94] "We have really no right",[95] says Campenhausen, to speak of a "Bishop" James, unless retrospectively using terminology from the second century.[96] We will return to this.

Concerning the historical "reminiscences" in the sources of the *Pseudo-Clementina,* however, Schöps has convincingly

---

[88] H. v. Campenhausen: *Die Nachfolge des Jakobus* in *Zts. f. Kirchengesch.* (1950–1) 133 ff.

[89] 1 Cor. 15:7.   [90] H. v. Campenhausen: *op. cit.* 137.   [91] Gal. 1:19.

[92] Acts 8:11; 11:19.   [93] Acts 12:7.   [94] Acts 15:13; 21:18.

[95] H. v. Campenhausen: *op. cit.* 134.   [96] *Ibid.* 141.

proved how much they were determined by Ebionite tendencies. This applies especially to the "Preaching of Peter" with the related "Letter of Peter to James" and the "Adjuration" – that is to keep the contents a secret. These are the sections of the work which have been least touched up. They deal with the didactic presentation of a self-contained system of allegedly Petrine sermons upon a foundation of sectarian (Ebionite) Scripture interpretation – "based upon the fiction that Peter had been obliged to render an account of his missionary activity every year to James".[97] The alleged letter of Peter to James "reproduces the Ebionite version of history as it appeared in retrospect after the disputes in the original congregation over the Law and with Paul". Peter himself is elevated as the representative of the Law in the gospel and "the whole thing is a Petrine – that is Ebionite – *apologia* against Paul and his adherents – that is the emerging early Catholic Church".[98] In this Peter does, it is true, possess a privileged position as the enemy of all "heresies", that is of the Gentile-Christian Catholic Church; and since Paul has sown his weeds far and wide Peter, too, has to follow the Pauline missionary routes to the communities in order to reclaim them for Jewish-Christianity; James, however, is, for the Judaistic version of history, the true head of "authentic Christianity" because he is said to have demanded circumcision of all Christians – and so on. Significant for the historical "reliability" of the Ebionite James – "traditions", indeed for their, "degree of impertinence" – to use Harnack's description[99]–, is the account of the commissioning apparitions at Easter in the

---

[97] H. J. Schöps: *op. cit.* 53. [98] *Ibid.* 119f.
[99] A. v. Harnack in: *Berl. S.-Ber.* 1922, 67.

Ebionite Gospel, in contrast to 1 Cor. 15:3ff. There James is the first to receive the calling of the Risen Lord and thus becomes leader of the Church. Accordingly, the Clementine source assigns to James the primacy in the early Church; and "whoever succeeds him" has a claim to the same.[100] Paul, on the other hand, is "the hostile man" – a reversal of Gal. 4:16.

It is worth noting in this connection that the notion of succession in the central episcopal office was accepted also by the Judaistic Church. When their first bishop, James, was killed by the Jews in 62 or 66[101], he seems to have been succeeded by another kinsman of Jesus, Simon bar Cleopas, who later at the time of the Jewish revolt led the exodus to Pella in East Jordania, and then returned to Jerusalem to be crucified in the year 107 – according to Hegesippus.[102] If not in his time, then during the episcopate of his successor the former tension with the Gentile-Christians may have led to an actual split, whereupon the Ebionites produced their own scriptures as an instrument of polemic. The third bishop – said to be Judas – lived through the revolt of bar Kochba (132–5) which brought an end to the existence of the Jewish-Christian community in Jerusalem. The severe attitude of the Epistle of Barnabas does seem to presuppose the separation from Jewish-Christianity. The main body of the sect – about a hundred thousand strong – lived from then on in East Jordania, also in Caesarea and in the neighbouring Syria. In the fourth-fifth century they gradually disappeared as a separate group.

[100] *Recogn.* 4, 35; *Hom.* 17, 13–20.
[101] Josephus reports this in *Antiquities* 20, 9, and so does Hegesippus in Eusebius *H.E.* II, 23, 11f.
[102] *Op. cit.*

To sum up: the research on the Clementine material as a whole, and particularly the work of H. J. Schöps and H. v. Campenhausen show that the Ebionite sources of the so-called Clement "are not to be taken seriously as historical sources for the apostolic age; rather, they are tendencious portrayals only valuable as giving information about the viewpoint of their own faction".[103] Their Judaistic slant probably came from the Jerusalem mother community but they organized themselves into a separate church, justifying their apostolic character by going back to James whom they "wanted to set . . . above Peter and all the rest of the apostles . . . ."[104] Their precursors are the pharisaical Jewish-Christians described in Acts 15:5, with whom the Apostle of the Gentiles had to contend in all of his communities, and who, following the Jewish school of Shammai, demanded circumcision before baptism of all Christians.

The rite of the Jewish "proselyte baptism"[105] has been preserved.

With regard to the Clementine fiction, as we have already said, the Catholic editor of the sources tried to erase the Ebionite traces in his models and bring them into harmony with biblical tradition. To make doubly sure, he fused Ebionite wisdom teaching with an *apologia* denouncing belief in fate, invented the frame-work of a *roman à clef*, the hero of which was given the exalted name of Clement of Rome, a youth in search of truth who in the end became the (allegedly immediate) successor of the first apostle, Peter, in the see of Rome. In this guise, graced with the name of Clement, this work became popular

[103] H. J. Schöps: *op. cit.* 439.   [104] H. v. Campenhausen: *op. cit.* 137.
[105] In the preface to the tractate *Gerim,* edited and expounded by G. Polster in: *Angelus* II (1926) 2–17.

throughout the ancient Christian world. Epiphanius, who was also able to get hold of the sources, had his suspicions, but consoled himself with the explanation that the work of the venerable author had been forged later by the Ebionites to serve their own ends.[106]

Hence, the early speculations of various writers[107] and

---

[106] Epiphanius: *Haer.* 29–30.

[107] Ed. Meyer: *Ursprung u. Anfänge* III (1923) 225 f.; K. Holl: *Ges. Aufsätze* II (1928) 49; E. Lohmeyer: *Gottesknecht und Davidssohn* (1945) 150. E. Stauffer takes up a special position (*Zum Kalifat des Jakobus* in *Zts. f. Religions- und Geistesgesch.* 1952, 193 ff.). According to him, James was designated "in a certain sense" successor to Peter, by Peter himself when he fled. He was elevated to the position of "leading man in the leading church of Christendom" and felt himself to be a kind of "president of the great sanhedrin of Christendom", with his seat in Jerusalem. His kinship with Jesus and the distinction conferred by the Easter apparition appealed to his deeply Judaistic cast of mind as supports for his claim. It is true that "Jesus thought in another fashion" but early Christianity, he affirms, "ignored Jesus' thought and intentions in an amazing number of points" – James himself serves as case of this very thing. There is, however, insufficient biblical foundation for the almost Ebionite exaggerated characterization of James. That the author of the Epistle of James felt himself to be the "Prince of Christendom" does not appear from the epistle itself; and Acts 21:25 does not prove that James "bound the Gentile-Christians with a Jewish food-taboo in addition to the three apostolic decrees" – quite the contrary. It is as impossible to affirm that the geographical Jerusalem with its Jewish-Christian senate carried more weight in the Church at large and with the author of Acts than the authority of the Twelve or the "right of supervision of the original apostles", as to say that the collection for the poor of Jerusalem is a proof of the "supreme juridical status of Jerusalem within the whole Church". (J. Weiss) But this is precisely what is happening when it is said that Paul is summoned before James and his senate in Acts 21:18, and that "we do not hear any more about the Twelve thereafter". This looks as though the original apostles have lost their authority and James has taken their place.

finally those of Cullmann on the primacy of James may be reduced to their true proportions. The other early Christian witnesses cited by Cullmann, even with the addition of his Pseudo-Clementine swallow do not make a Jacobean summer. On this issue, neither Clement of Alexandria[108] nor Hegesippus[109] have the status of independent witnesses. They judge the Judaistic historical legends by the same sources as the Pseudo-Clement.[110] Clement of Alexandria's suggestion that "Peter, James, and John, after the ascension of Jesus, renounced the pre-eminent position and chose James the Just as the Bishop of Jerusalem" would certainly have been just as incredible to Pseudo-Clement as to Cullmann himself.[111] For Clement of Alexandria did believe in the primacy of Peter [112] and in the "earthly hierarchy in the Church as a reflection of the heavenly hierarchy".[113] The gossip of Hegesippus is selfcontradictory; according to him on one occasion James took over the Church "with the apostles",[114] on another, "from the apostles".[115] He allows his imagination free rein: James is "the bulwark of the people",[116] "only he is permitted to enter the Holy of Holies in the prescribed linen vestment in order to make perpetual intercession for the sins of his people."[117] From this it is only one step to the fantasy of James as "High-Priest".[118]

---

[108] In Eusebius: *H.E.* II, 1, 3.　[109] In Eusebius: *H.E.* II, 23.
[110] See H. J. Schöps: *op. cit.* 413 ff.　[111] *Peter* p. 230 n. 25.
[112] Clement of Alexandria: *Quis dives* 21.
[113] *Strom.* VI, 13,107.　[114] Eusebius: *H.E.* II, 23, 4.
[115] *Ibid.* 23, 1.　[116] *Ibid.* 23, 7.　[117] *Ibid.* 23, 6.
[118] In Epiphanius: *Haer.* 78, 9. A. v. Harnack (*Chronologie* I, 186) and H. v. Campenhausen (*op. cit.* 137[27]) do not agree about whether Epiphanius can be traced back to Hegesippus.

All in all Cullmann certainly cannot take it amiss if we do not feel constrained by the sources of the Clementine fiction, with its Pope of Ebionite imagination, to correct the credible primitive Christian tradition. In the New Testament, as we have seen, the supposed clues are missing – unless we adopt the Ebionite position. But if, with Cullmann, we do assume that James replaced Peter – what then? What would be gained? The confirmation of the principle of succession. Upon Peter followed James – and upon James followed . . . ?

2. The Biblical meaning of apostolic succession

Protestant theology cannot accept a succession of the apostles in general, or of Peter as the first, either from Matthew 16:17ff. and 18:18 or anywhere else. Cullmann argues particularly impressively and I summarize his reasoning as follows:

1. Peter is the first apostle. He received the primacy as an apostle or in connection with the apostolic dignity.[119] To be an apostle means to have been directly commissioned by the Lord as a witness to Christ who proclaims the reign of God, who suffered, was raised from the dead and is exalted at the right hand of God. Peter shares the dignity of an apostle with others, as first amongst them. Together they constitute the "foundation"[120] of the Church, "the foundations and wall of the holy city".[121] As apostles, they have no successors: "At the moment when Peter receives the promise of being the rock of the coming Church, he is addressed as one of the Twelve . . . the apostolic

---

[119] *Peter* p. 222f. [120] Eph. 2:20. [121] Apoc. 21:14.

office, particularly that of the Twelve, is a unique office not to be repeated."[122]

2. Jesus desires to build his Church upon the rock of Peter but "it is only the work of building which belongs to an unlimited future, not the laying of the foundation of the rock on which it is built!"[123] and if the "building" includes the post-Petrine age also, "this would mean only that the unique mission as rock which the historical Peter fulfils in the redemptive history is of such a character that its unique effectiveness continues even beyond his death, so that the historical Peter – and not any successors – would be and remain the foundation even in this unlimited further building."[124] "To be sure there must be guarantors, watchmen, shepherds, interpreters in the Church" but they may not apply the saying about the rock to themselves: "They are indispensable materials of which Christ makes use in the further building of his Church."[125] Peter and the apostles (and the prophets, according to Ephesians 2:20) are the foundation. Upon this rises up the holy temple of "living stones".[126] Peter remains "in a certain respect the archetype and example for all future church leadership"; and what later ages build up are not – following the sense of the biblical image – additional "layers" or "storeys" completing what was left "unfinished", but are in the purely chronological sense the new generations, while amidst the changes of time the self-same apostolic-Petrine foundation remains.[127]

3. This, however, shows us only the negative side of the biblical-theological reality. Even if the apostolic function and

---

[122] *Peter* p. 220.   [123] *Ibid.* p. 214.   [124] *Ibid.* p. 215.
[125] *Ibid.* p. 227.   [126] 1 Pet. 2:5.   [127] *Peter* pp. 228–9.

the office of the rock are not transferable, "the functions of leading and doing missionary work do indeed continue".[128] Presbyters (elders) = *episkopoi* (watchmen, bishops) take the place of the apostles "and we may call them successors, even if this expression opens the way to misunderstandings". What is meant are ecclesiastical "officers", "elders" who "lead the flock" – as we hear in Acts 14:23; 20:17ff. "The apostles gave over to those men the leadership, but not their own apostolic office."[129] These are the "beginnings of a so-called apostolic succession". The term appears ambiguous and misleading – though we might note that Cullmann has interpreted it correctly.

Let us pause to enquire – with regard to 3 first of all: is there any Catholic theologian or educated layman who would differ from what Cullmann has shown to be in accordance with the facts of the New Testament? Certainly not. We need only refer to B. Bartmann in his *Dogmatik*.[130] He makes the following distinctions between apostolic and episcopal function.

a) "Apostles" hold a world-wide commission, episcopal "successors" are set over particular ecclesiastical areas.

b) The "apostles" were witnesses of Christ and the direct recipients of divine revelation, their episcopal "successors" have only to preserve what they have received and hand it on.

c) The individual apostles personally possessed the *charisma* of truth, the bishops possess it only as a body.

With this we might also compare G. Söhngen: "Truly the bishops are successors of the apostles, without themselves being

---

[128] *Ibid.* p. 220; p. 224f.   [129] *Ibid.* p. 224.
[130] B. Bartmann: *Dogmatik* II ([8]1932) 157.

apostles . . . the Pope is indeed the successor of the apostle Peter, without himself being an apostle."[131]

Whether the theological term "apostolic succession" – a later historical invention – is the most perfect term conceivable is a debatable question. The important thing is what the term denotes, the meaning of the phrase; and Cullmann himself has recognized the biblical sense. The New Testament leaves us in no doubt on this point, that definite responsibilities for the Church "continue" from the apostles' time onwards. And the Pastoral Epistles are not the first place where this appears. The Protestant theologian W. Mundle notes, with reference to the Acts of the Apostles, that besides the notion of apostolic authority, "the notion of the 'apostolic succession' dominates the historical picture presented in the Acts of the Apostles".[132] "Those who held the apostolic episcopal office, who finally became the leaders of the Church, did not set themselves up to be apostles. They are only the successors, at most the representatives of the apostles. As such they remain bound by the original apostolic word and testimony embodied in the New Testament."[133] "The institution of ecclesiastical offices goes back to the authority of the apostles", and those who hold such office "hold their position of authority in fee from the apostles".[134]

This quite corresponds with the Catholic view, as does the observation of Johannes Munck[135] that the assistants and representatives of the apostles in the congregations – the "seven" for

---

[131] G. Söhngen: *Die Einheit der Theologie* (1952) 307.
[132] W. Mundle in: *Zts. nt. W.* 1928, 41.
[133] H. v. Campenhausen: *Kirchl. Amt* 25.
[134] W. Mundle: *op. cit.* 40.
[135] Joh. Munck in: *Mélanges off. à M. Goguel* (1950) 170.

the Hellenistic group in Jerusalem, the "elders" of the Jewish-Christian group and of the Pauline congregations in Ephesus, and so on – "already existed beside the apostles and did not take up their responsibility only on the death of the apostles". They were not, that is, merely posthumous successors, as the terminology might suggest, but simply lease-holders, sharers in responsibility for the Church in dependence upon the apostles.

An Anglican theologian, the present Archbishop of Canterbury, wrote about the apostolic succession[136]: "And the three meanings which have been assigned to the phrase 'Apostolic succession' all derive their significance from the Gospel. (i) The phrase is first of all used of the succession of Bishop to Bishop in office[137], . . . (ii) . . . of the functions wherein the Bishops succeed the Apostles[138]. . . (iii) for succession in grace[139], whereby grace is handed down from the Apostles through the Bishops from one generation to another. . . . Apostolic succession in this third sense is not an isolated channel of grace but always an organ of the grace of our Lord Jesus Christ working through the Body as a whole. Every act of grace is our Lord's act and the act of the whole Body . . . ."

---

[136] A. M. Ramsey: *Apostolic Succession* in Zoellner-Stählin: *Die Kirche Jesu Christi* (1937) 179 ff. A most important work is the Anglican collection by K. E. Kirk: *The Apostolic Ministry*, 1946, containing contributions by A. M. Farrer: *The Ministry in the N.T.*, 113 ff. and by Gregory Dix: *The Ministry in the Early Church*, 183 ff. The main theme is that the episcopal structure was, from the start, not only of the *bene esse* but of the *esse* of the Church.

[137] Irenaeus: *Adv. Haer.* III, 3, 6; 4, 1.

[138] Hippolytus: *Philos.,* Introduction.

[139] Indicated by the invocation of the Holy Spirit: Acts 13:3; 1 Tim. 4:14; 2 Tim. 1:6.

Correspondingly, the Petrine succession in the Catholic Church is not conceived as though with a change of person a new "rock" always replaces the earlier one. What is handed on is the function of the central element of ecclesiastical authority with the purpose of "strengthening" all of the brethren and of protecting the unity of all in the spirit of our Lord's sacerdotal prayer in John 17.

3. Did Jesus and his apostles envisage the apostolic succession for the future?

First of all it is certain, and Cullmann readily admits, that Jesus envisaged a future of undetermined length ahead of the Church[140]. The view of A. Schweitzer and others that Jesus expected his return to coincide with his death "cannot be supported by any text" and is positively contradicted by a series of passages which point to the future.[141]

The definitive elucidation of the "eschatological problem" emerges, however, in my opinion, out of the passage in the prophecy of Daniel 7 itself which Jesus and the synoptists including Paul and John had in mind in their prophetic pronouncements. "The Son of Man will come upon the clouds of heaven" (about which event, according to Matthew 10:23; 16:28; 24:34; 26:64, Jesus speaks as though of an imminent reality, "from now on" beginning to emerge) is not only reproduced analogously in the parallel texts Mark 9:1 and Luke 9:27 in the periphrasis "The kingdom of God comes with power" but this meaning is already expressly given by Daniel himself and originates there. In Daniel,

[140] *Peter* p. 204 ff.   [141] Mark 2:18 ff.; 13:8–13; Matt. 28:20; Luke 22:19; John 2:19–22; 4:23 35 ff.

the coming "Son of Man" is already an image of the conquest of the kingdoms of this world by the coming imperishable kingdom of the holy people – see Daniel 7:13, 16, 17. And Paul too, no matter how much his human outlook may have been tinged by rabbinic influences, knows of the day "when he shall come to be glorified in his saints and to be made wonderful in all them who believed . . . ."[142] He knows, that is, that the coming of the Christ, his "return" in the power of the Spirit and, according to John 14–17, his "remaining" with his disciples, is realized in the faith-experience of his holy people.[143]

When Cullmann emphasizes that the apostolic office is unique and non-recurrent he is opening doors that were never closed. In an incidental remark he admits that this is "quite strongly stressed" by Catholic theology.[144] The Roman, Eastern, and Anglican Churches when they refer to "apostolic succession" affirm nothing but this: that certain powers, certain functions of preaching and administering the sacraments and of enforcing discipline within the community – "binding and loosing" in Jesus' sense – are handed on. Cullmann affirms this as we have seen. He cites, moreover, a number of Protestant theologians and might have cited many more of these[145] who part company with theo-

---

[142] See Dan. 7:13 16 27.
[143] Literary discussion of the eschatological problem seems to have missed the explanation given by Daniel 7 itself. I owe this suggestion to Bert Zwicky (synodal counsellor, Herzogen-Buchensee-Bern).
[144] *Peter* p. 224 n. 10.
[145] O. Scheel in: *Theol. Stud. u. Krit.* 1912, 432; Ed. Schweizer and Ph. H. Menoud (quoted by Cullmann); and also K. Holl: *Ges. Aufs.* II (1928) 44ff.; E. Stauffer: *Theologie des N. T.* (41948) 17f.; the joint authors of compilation by Zoellner-Stählin; Joh. Munck: *op. cit.* 169f. (see note 229); F. C. Grant: *An Introduction* (1950) 271ff.

logians such as R. Sohm and E. Brunner, protagonists of a purely charismatic Church.

The principle of succession in responsible ministry within the community was in the air: "even in the ancient world of the Bible it played an important part".[146] The office of mediator which Moses received from God's hand is unique, yet he appointed Josue to be his successor.[147] The teachers in Israel "sit in Moses' chair" and Jesus did not depart at all from this principle – quite the opposite in fact.[148] The apostles emerged from this world and, following the mind of Jesus, used the thought-structure of the ancient people of God to apply it to the institutions of the Church. As the result of a series of studies,[149] it has been recognized that "before the youthful Christianity appeared in the Hellenistic world, the basic features of its nature were fashioned from Palestinian Judaism".[150] Christian public worship "grew out of Jewish worship".[151] Christology is something new, the rest is "an inheritance from the synagogue".[152] The "binding

---

[146] E. Stauffer: *op, cit.* 17, 215 f. Cf. W. Bacher: *Tradition u. Tradenten in Palästina* (1914); J. Ranf: *Der Ursprung des kath. Traditionsprinzips* (1931) 152 ff.

[147] Num. 27:18 ff.   [148] Matt. 23:6.

[149] G. Dalmann: *Die Worte Jesu* (1898); A. Schlatter: *Die Kirche Jerusalems* (1898); G. Löschke: *Jüdisches u. Heidnisches im christlichen Kult* (1898); R. Bultmann: *Gesch. der synoptischen Trad.* (1921); A. Baumstark: *Vom geschichtl. Werden der Liturgie* (1923); J. Jeremias: *Golgotha u. der heilige Felsen* (1926); J. Dupont: *Gnosis* (1949); A. Oepke: *Das neue Gottesvolk* (1950) 180 ff.; F. C. Grant: *An Introduction to N. T. Thought* (1950) 59 f.; 268 f.; 295; E. Stauffer in: *Zts. f. Religions- und Geistesgeschichte* (1952) 193 ff.

[150] G. Kittel: *Die Probleme* . . . (1926) 2.

[151] P. Wendland: *Die hell.-röm. Kultur* (1912) 225.

[152] A. Baumstark: *op. cit.* 13.

and loosing" by those in authority is a rabbinic technical term. The "imposition of hands" as a sign of the handing on of authority goes back to Old Testament models.[153] The celebration of the Eucharist by one presbyter-bishop and not by anyone who chose to preside, arose from the necessary connection, indicated in the Epistle to the Hebrews, between sacrifice and priesthood.[154] What is celebrated is the sacerdotal sacrifice of Jesus by his priestly people under the leadership of the presbyter. It is the celebration of the Eucharist, as St. Paul "received it from the Lord" along with the bases of the gospel-preaching, and delivered to the primitive Church.[155]

At this point we may be permitted a comment upon the view put forward by C. H. Turner[156] and E. Caspar[157] that during the first three centuries "succession" means, not the sequence of persons direct, but the inner unity of doctrine, its "passing on" or, rather, its "continuing reception from hand to hand". What is now passed on is, "the pure doctrine", once maintained upon Moses' chair, now, in the new Covenant, upon the apostolic *cathedra*. It is clear that this interpretation by no means disposes of the principle of succession but, on the contrary, partly gives it a spiritual foundation. Nonetheless, this interpretation does seem to restrict the historical circumstances and take only some of them into consideration. If it can be shown that, according to early Christian concepts, the valid celebration of sacramental worship

---

[153] Num. 8:10f.; 27:218.

[154] J. M. Nielen: *Gebet u. Gottesdienst im N.T.* (1937) 321.

[155] 1 Cor. 11:23; cf. 15:3ff.

[156] C. H. Turner in H. B. Swete: *Essay on the Early History of the Church* (1918) 207ff.

[157] E. Caspar: *Die älteste röm. Bischofsliste* (1926) 233ff.; 443ff.

and the responsibility for discipline within the community is no less tied to the leadership of the presbyter-bishop than is the normative tradition of doctrine, then the one-sidedness of the thesis of Turner-Caspar concerning the restriction to "pure doctrine" is proved.[158]

According to Scripture, the function of the elders *(episkopoi)* embraces both teaching and community discipline,[159] both liturgy and sacraments[160] and pastoral care in the general sense of the pastoral ministry.[161] In the conflict with Marcion, Montanus, and the Gnostics, it was obviously a matter of countering the notions of unrestrained philosophy, prophecy, and mysticism by emphasizing the pure tradition of doctrine. Due to religious awe, the sacramental mystery was kept out of the debate with outsiders. For the Pastoral Epistles the significance of ecclesiastical authority lay principally in the safe-guarding of the apostolic tradition against the threats to the faith from heretical gnosis. "Ordination appears indeed as the indispensable source of strength for the exercise of spiritual office" and the concepts "tradition" and "reception" of the heritage entrusted – *paradosis* and *diadoche* – received a "sharply defined meaning" in contrast to the gnostic appeal to an esoteric apostolic tradition.[162] Thus it is with Papias and Cle-

---

[158] Cf. F. Probst: *Lehre u. Gebet in den ersten zwei Jahrh.* (1871); J. M. Nielen: *op. cit.* (n. 248).

[159] Acts. 15:23–9; 16:9; 21:18 25.

[160] James 5:14.

[161] Acts 20:17–31. Cf. F. C. Grant: *An Introduction* (1950) 42, 275 ff.

[162] H. v. Campenhausen: *Kirchl. Amt* 169 f.; 172 f., where the view is stated that the evolution of the precise concept of succession (with resulting lists of bishops by Hegesippus and others) goes back to models in Hellenistic-gnostic philosophical circles. E. Kohlmeyer (in *Zts. f. Rechtsgesch.* 1952, Can. section 1 ff.) and especially E. Stauffer (in *Zts. f. Reli-*

ment of Alexandria who rightly account such prominent presbyters as Polycarp to be specially endowed witnesses to the true
tradition, because they were immediate pupils of the apostles.
But that is only one side of the official responsibility, which came
to be stressed by reason of the circumstances of the period. In the
Church's life "the word and the bread of life" were both equally
important: the liturgical direction of the celebration of the Eucharist was part of the essential duty of the holy ministery. The Acts
of the Apostles and 1 Peter already have an ecclesiastical office
in mind, the duties of which include "preaching, admonition,
direction, discipline, care of the flock, and representation of the
community in worship".[163]

According to Clement of Rome, the most important post-
apostolic witness in the first century, it is the presbyter-bishops
who "offer the sacrificial gifts" (44:4), that is, who lead the celebration of the liturgy; and "their activity from the beginning
must have possessed a comprehensive character".[164] The Epistle
of Clement declares the sacral status of the office to be particularly necessary for the liturgical duties; and this principle can
scarcely be regarded as a sudden innovation. "The assumption
that the spiritual leaders and directors of public worship originally changed at will is an arbitrary hypothesis."[165] Ignatius of

gions- und Geistesgeschichte 1952, 207 ff.) have opposed this view with
convincing proofs. They affirm that the whole thing is a sound Jewish
tradition. Complete lists of the sequence of high-priests in Jerusalem were
kept, and "the Jews argued with proofs from the Law and from the succession of high-priests" (Josephus: Ant. 13, 3, 4).
[163] Ibid. 327.   [164] Ibid. 92.
[165] Ibid. 100. If, however, on Campenhausen's view, Clement does indeed trace the office of bishop back to the apostles, thus justifying the
"apostolic succession" (v. C. 93), but at the same time pays "no atten-

Antioch felt the Church to be a living mystery of unity in Christ. Its essence, "spirit and flesh", only appeared in the leadership of tion at all to the main matter, that is its relation to the tradition of doctrine" (v. C. 172), then we must ask by what norm one official function is described here as the "main matter" in contrast to others of secondary importance. H. v. Campenhausen himself, however, does not maintain the distinction consistently. According to him, the most important post-apostolic witnesses (Pastoral Epistles, Clement, Ignatius, Polycarp) understood by sacred tradition "traditional doctrine and sacerdotal activities" amongst which they accounted liturgical duties of special importance, then stressed increasingly their responsibility "as guardians and witnesses of the true tradition" against the Gnostics (v. Campenhausen 166). Clement, the Pastoral Epistles, and Ignatius' Epistles make it clear that ecclesiastical authority knew itself to be responsible for Church order and discipline (from the beginning). In short, the distinction of a "main matter" from secondary matters seems somewhat artificial in this context. That Clement took a special interest in Church order appears from his letter. He had to make the Corinthians sharply aware of the importance of Church order (and subordination) because this was threatened. It is basically misguided to conclude that a notion is absent (in this case that of the tradition of doctrine) because it is not stressed. This applies to v. Campenhausen's remark concerning Ignatius also. Ignatius, who manifestly exalts the episcopal office, "knows no grace of order and no longer reminds the bishop, in the manner of the Pastoral Epistles, of his ordination" (v. C. 114). As if one could or would expound the whole of dogma on every occasion! It is as false as if one were to say that v. Campenhausen himself wishes to imply a disregard for the Trinity, justification by faith, or membership in the mystical Body, because he does not write about these things in his book. As for Clement, he is anxious to trace authority within the community back to the apostles (42 and 44), and to do this he refers plainly to 1 Cor. 16:15ff., as elsewhere he uses 1 Cor. 13:1ff. (Clem. 47:1 = 1 Cor. 1:10ff.; Clem. 49:5 = 1 Cor. 13:1ff.). The "first-fruits" of Corinth, mentioned by name, he takes to be presidents, and the Pauline phrase: "they have devoted themselves to the holy ministry" does not refer to the free charismatic ministry. Paul means that they were prepared to accept the highly responsible and dangerous office of authority (See *Biblica* 1939, 276ff.).

the bishop within the circle of his presbyters – "apart from these no church deserves the name".[166] With these, however, are joined all the "God-bearers" within that unity which the bishop represents. For Justin, too, it is just as obvious that Eucharistic worship is celebrated only in union with the bishop – the presiding member pronouncing the solemn prayer of thanksgiving.[167] Concerning the *Didache* or *Teaching of the Twelve Apostles,* A. Arnold falls into an error in his otherwise excellent study, "The origin of the Last Supper". He asserts that "a prophet" says "the thanksgiving prayer of consecration, the content and significance of which appears from Justin's first *Apology*".[168] If that was the case, then, according to early Christian practice, anyone might in principle preside over the celebration of the Eucharist within the circle of brethren. But there a misunderstanding is involved. The passage cited in chapter 10 runs: "Let the prophets give thanks – *eucharistein* – as much as they please." This does not refer to the celebration of the Eucharist but generally to the meeting in the course of which the *agape* took place and when, following apostolic custom,[169] either before or after the Lord's Supper, "all are permitted to prophesy in turn so that all may learn, and receive encouragement". Justin, however, is speaking exclusively of the celebration of the Eucharist which in that time was no longer joined to the *agape,* the social meal; and it is of the Eucharist that he writes: "He who presides offers up prayers and thanksgivings – *eucharistias* – according to his ability" – an allu-

---

[166] Ignatius: *Trall.* 3, 1; cf. *Philad.* 4; *Smyrn.* 8 f. *Ancient Christian Writers,* 1946 (London) Vol. I. p. 76.
[167] Justin: *Apol.* I, 65 ff.
[168] A. Arnold: *Der Ursprung des christl. Abendmahls* (1937) 110.
[169] 1 Cor. 12:1–11 and 14:31.

sion to the personal form of the prayer. It is wrong to conclude that the significance is similar since the same word – *eucharistein* – *eucharistias* – was used. As is well known, the word has a wider and a narrower meaning depending upon the context. In the *Didache* it clearly means thanksgiving in the setting of the *agape;* in Justin it has the narrower meaning of Eucharistic thanksgiving, of the prayer of consecration within the canon of the Mass. Neither in that ancient Church document nor anywhere else is there a mention of a "thanksgiving prayer of consecration by a prophet".

Let us return to succession in office. Concerning the *episkopoi* – overseers, bishops –, a term which in the Pauline period and in the time of Clement of Rome towards the end of the first century means the same as "presbyters" or "elders", we note that the function which they performed in the community had a certain correspondence with the Jewish elders. Its New Testament significance can be deduced from the Acts and the Epistles of the apostles.[170] The presbyter-bishop watched above all over people and regulations. Occasionally Jesus himself appears as bishop – "Shepherd and bishop of your souls";[171] otherwise the concept is used of those who preside over the congregation.[172] Who appointed these possessors of authority in the New Testament? According to Acts 14:23, it was the apostles – in consultation with the congregation. This must be our normal assumption, especially as it is confirmed in the Pastoral Epistles. In the Epistle to the Philippians 1:1 the bishops, too, are appointed by Paul and are to rule according to his spirit. According to Acts 20:28, in this

[170] See K. H. Rengstorf: *Die apost. Sukz.* in Zoellner-Stählin: *op. cit.* 192.
[171] 1 Pet. 2:25.   [172] Acts 14:23; 20:17ff.; Phil. 1:1 etc.

function the apostle is a mediator of the Holy Spirit, for, according to the biblical notion, all "building up" of the Church[173]
is effected in the Holy Spirit.[174] The Holy Spirit moulds the congregation, controls the apostles and those whom they commission,[175] not *vis-à-vis* the Church, but on its behalf and hence with
the moral co-operation of the congregation:[176] "The congregation elect the office-bearers, the apostles ordain them."[177]

And what do we find in the Bible concerning the unique
"foundation" of the Church? Whether it is Christ himself[178] or
the apostles and prophets[179] or Peter[180] who is designated thus,
in each case we are dealing with a Scripture saying with a spiritual meaning. B. Bartmann[181] points this out emphatically. In a
physical building the parts remain the same until they gradually
decay. The Church is not made of stones but of living people of
whom Peter, the rock, is one – even if we want to think, in
terms of the presumably Galilean Aramaic, of a solid rock hewn
out to form a rock-bottom foundation.[182] The Church is a living
building in the Holy Spirit, its individual members are "living
stones" in the Holy Spirit.[183] By the necessity of nature, in such

[173] 1 Cor. 14:12.   [174] 1 Cor. 12:14.; Eph. 4:3; 2 Tim. 1:7.
[175] Titus 1:5.   [176] Acts 1:15; 1 Tim. 3:1ff.; Tit. 1:5ff.
[177] K. H. Rengstorf in Zoellner-Stählin: *Die Kirche Jesu Christi* (1937) 192.
Of the historical circumstances of the early Church it is said that the
congregation co-operated in choosing their own office-bearers. This does
not imply that the congregation had a right to demand the ordination
of their own candidate, but that, following the concept of the people of
God, the rulers (apostles and their successors) acted as far as possible in
unison with the Christian people, and did not look upon them as an
object standing "over against" them.
[178] 1 Cor. 3:11.   [179] Eph. 2:20.   [180] Matt. 16:18.
[181] B. Bartmann: *Dogmatik* II (⁸1932) 171.
[182] J. Horst in: *Zts. f. syst. Theol.* 1943, 139.   [183] 1 Pet. 2:5.

a building there is a renewal of persons, at the foundation as well
as in the superstructure, for the very reason that they are men,
"spiritual" not material stones.

As we see again from Ephesians 2:20, the Church is "built
upon the foundation of the apostles and prophets". The two
groups together form the foundation, that is they are basic,
essential for ever. It is true that apostles are unique as apostles, but
not as "responsible leaders" of the Church. They are placed beside the "prophets", who in the New Testament are preachers,
moved by the free impulse of the Holy Spirit. Because these prophets were part of the "foundation", that is, belonged exclusively to the founding period, can we say that they are perhaps
"unique" in the sense that there may not be any more of them?
In that case Protestantism with its strong emphasis on the proph-
etic-charismatic element would put an end to itself. If the
prophets have their counterparts in every age, so have the apostles. According to Ephesians 2, the free charismatic ministry and
the official ministry are both essential to the Church's mission as
instrument of the kingdom of God in the world. In other words:
"the general and the special priesthood", "the responsible leadership and the mission of the laity" complement one another.
For the official ministry it is necessary that a person be regularly
appointed – *rite vocatus* – not called simply by charismatic inspiration and preparation as a voluntary witness to the Spirit. Fail-
ing that, the Church would rest, not "upon the apostles and
prophets", but only upon prophets.

Let us consider further: Jesus appointed the apostles for the
sake of the coming reign of God, hence as a provision for the
needs of the growing Church, especially in the time when he
himself will no longer be visible upon earth. By his intention

they were to be his delegates, the representatives of him who sent them: "Who hears you hears me",[184] and "Who receives you receives me."[185] Their mission beyond the time of Jesus' physical presence on earth is described in the parable in Matthew 25:14ff. according to which "a man going into a far country called his servants and delivered to them his goods; and he gave them authority during the time of his absence, to one he gave five talents, and to another two, and to another one".[186] The parable expresses our Lord's mind without ambiguity: from the time of his departure onwards, plenipotentiaries, his "representatives", were to have responsibility in various degrees, in his name. The commission is given for the time when he will be absent, that is for the "latter days". The apostles understood what he meant and accordingly appointed other men to act when they were absent. These were to be their representatives so that the flock would never be left without a shepherd.[187] "As long as the Lord is invisible with the Father, they are in the place of disciples", "servants" answerable to him.[188] Jesus had no "successor" as Messiah, but he called the Twelve. As apostles in the specific sense these have no successors; but they have successors as shepherds of the flock, in terms of the commission "go and make disciples of all nations ... until the end of the world".[189] As Cullmann says elsewhere,[190] this commission was "the comprehensive founding of the Church". And because the commission endures "until the end of the world", it does not apply to the

---

[184] Luke 10:16.   [185] Matt. 10:40.

[186] Matt. 25:14ff., following German version.   [187] Cf. Mark 6:34.

[188] A. F. C. Vilmar: *Die Lehre vom geistlichen Amt* (1870).

[189] Matt. 28:19f.

[190] Cullmann: *Königsherrschaft Christi u. Kirche im N.T.* (1941) 9.

apostles personally, for they do not live for ever, but to them as bearers of Jesus' authority. And so it is Jesus' intention that there should always be bearers of this apostolic authority. Consequently others will have to come and take over from the apostles. "One man soweth and it is another that reapeth" – the earlier generation works and a later comes along and "enters into their labours".[191]

With reference to the continuance of the apostolic office, therefore, two things must be distinguished.[192] First, a ministry as authentic first witnesses and bearers of revelation. This pertains to Peter and the apostles alone. Only they can say: "That which was from the beginning, which we have heard, which we have seen with our eyes, which we have looked upon and our hands have handled, of the word of life; ... we declare unto you; that you may have fellowship with us, and our fellowship may be with the Father and with his Son Jesus Christ."[193] The apostles alone are immediate witnesses of revelation and after them none can preach any new revelation. But, secondly, Peter and the other apostles also receive the commission to make disciples, and this commission extends into time and it is taken over from them by other bearers of full authority. Continuing leadership is part of the continuing Church. Those who come later must hand on the teaching of the apostles. Apostles and bishop – *presbyteroi* – *episkopoi* – are "links in the same chain".[194] The chain of authority extends from the apostles right down through time. The

---

191 John 4:38.
192 See R. Baumann: *Des Petrus Bekenntnis u. Schlüssel* (1950) 17.
193 1 John 1:1–3.
194 K. H. Rengstorf in Kittel's *Th. Wb.* I, 430; likewise K. Müller, quoted by E. Caspar and R. Baumann *op. cit.* 135.

apostles as the first messengers and the bishops as their fully authorized representatives have something in common: both are "servants" in the sense of Jesus' parable, and the Scriptures call both, God's "stewards" – the apostles are so named in 1 Cor. 4:1; the bishops in Titus 1:7. The gradation of sharing in the dignity of Christ the "great Shepherd of the sheep",[195] the "Shepherd and bishop of your souls"[196] passes through the apostles, who can humbly refer to themselves as presbyters,[197] to the shepherds of the congregation who for their part, too, are bearers of sacred powers. God – Christ – the apostles – the bishops (elders) are "the links in the chain upon which the Church hangs".[198] Thus the office of bishop is the "continuance of the office of apostle in new circumstances".[199] As earlier, apostles had been necessary as Christ's representatives, so later, the bishops or elders came into being as representatives of their apostolic predecessors, just as necessary as these had been in their own time. That a book would be sufficient to preserve the unity of the flock was quite foreign to Jesus' thought, as we shall show later. The Church always faces the same conditions within itself and outside. Within is the Spirit and its organs, outside are "false prophets who seduce even the elect",[200] "ravening wolves who break into the flock".[201] Were the apostles not bound to take the precaution of appointing "shepherds", "watchmen" *(episkopoi)*, to accept responsibility for the flock? Did they not do this according to the mind of Christ?

[195] Heb. 13:20.   [196] 1 Pet. 2:25.
[197] 1 Pet. 5:1; 2 John 1.
[198] K. Müller quoted by R. Baumann: *op. cit.*
[199] K. H. Rengstorf in Zoellner-Stählin: *op. cit.* 188.
[200] Mark 13:12.   [201] Acts 20:29.

4. Are there other ways of transferring authority?

When thus Cullmann himself affirms that the apostles were succeeded by elders (bishops) to whom they "give over ... the leadership",[202] this is biblical truth in the narrower sense, and, for the period of transition from the apostolic to the post-apostolic age, supported in Acts 20:28–31, the Pastoral Epistles, and the Apostolic Fathers. When, however, he goes beyond this and, along with many others, asserts: "In what way the latter (those appointed by the apostles to preside) in turn are to follow one another, the New Testament does not say at all",[203] this statement is understandable in terms of the historical situation of Protestantism which has arisen apart from bishops, but it cannot be regarded as biblical.

True, we do not expect to find much in the apostolic writings – which were addressed to contemporaries – concerning the later handing on by the post-apostolic holders of authority to those who succeeded them, and what we do find will be indirect information. There is no theoretical statement about succession, for no one was writing a theological text-book; but there is enough said to allow the principle already realized in the transition from the apostles to bishops to be illustrated by concrete examples. And if it is true that we can deduce faith from prayer, the *lex credendi* from the *lex orandi,* then the same holds true of the *lex tradendi,* of the tradition of Church order inaugurated by the apostles.

First, in Acts 20:28, something fundamental is said concern-

[202] *Peter* p. 224.
[203] *Peter* p. 224 in agreement with the common Protestant thesis. See E. Schlink: *Theologie d. luth. Bekenntnisschriften* (1946) 334ff.

ing the handing on of authority: "the Holy Spirit" has "appointed the presbyter-bishops" as "guardians who must tend the Church of God". That the Holy Spirit is conferred with prayer and under the sign of "extending of hands" or "imposition of hands" is mentioned earlier in Acts 6:6; 14:23. In this way the manner and form of handing on authority along the chain of post-apostolic Church leaders is set down from the start.[204] It is the manner and form as founded by the spirit of tradition in the Palestinian world and taken over by Paul to such an extent that the Pastoral Epistles are only confirming what is already traditional usage. Hence, Titus, a pupil of Paul and now missionary legate, is told: "For this cause I left thee in Crete; that thou shouldest set in order the things that are wanting and shouldest ordain elders (presbyter-bishops) in every city, as I also appointed thee."[205] And the apostle exhorts Timothy, his other legate: "Impose not hands lightly upon any man; neither be partaker of other men's sins (that is, by so doing)."[206] The context suggests that most likely he has the ordination of presbyter-bishops in mind.[207] Timothy's own ordination by the laying on of the apostle's and presbyters' hands is mentioned in 1 Tim. 4:14 and 2 Tim. 1:6.

[204] F. C. Grant: *An Introduction* (1950) 276. E. Stauffer in *Zts. f. Religions-und Geistesgeschichte* 1952, 209 ff. shows that the transmission of authority by imposition of hands and installation in the *cathedra* is a continuation of traditional Jewish custom and cannot be a derivation from the post-apostolic age. The sharp hostility between Church and Synagogue anyhow excluded a dependence of that sort.

[205] Titus 1:5.   [206] 1 Tim. 5:22.

[207] And yet we must note that there are exegetes who understand 1 Tim. 5:22 to refer to the imposition of hands in forgiveness – B. J. Galtier, for example, in his most recent book: *Aux origines du Sacrement de pénitence* (1951).

Emil Brunner's judgment on apostolic succession is worth noting. "This theory ... doubtless ... not a pure fiction ... possessed at least a good *fundamentum in re*." "The bishops' lists of Hegesippus mentioned by Eusebius, (and before him by Irenaeus[208], on which especially the doctrine of apostolic succession is based, do not of course reach back with certainty to the apostolic age ... but there can be no doubt that certain congregations long remembered that their leaders had once been instituted by apostles; the Pastoral Epistles are to be valued as symptomatic of this growing interest in the apostolic succession."[209] Thus when Calvin gave the church in Geneva a constitution having a consistory of theologians and laymen, and derived this "correct" constitution from the New Testament, this is, according to Brunner, who argues of course not from Catholic premises – "an exegetical error".[210] The same writer says of the

---

[208] Irenaeus: *Adv. Haer.* III, 2, 3; Eusebius: *H. E.* IV, 22, 3.

[209] Emil Brunner: *The Misunderstanding of the Church* (1952) London, p. 79f. and 129.

[210] *Ibid.* 104. To be fair, however, something more has to be said. Not only did Calvin (*Inst.* IV 3–4) show the apostolic foundation of ecclesiastical authority, and desire to restore to the ministry, after its late medieval decline, the primitive Christian concept of "representation of Christ" on the one hand and of service to the congregation on the other; but Huguenot Calvinism, and the Second Helvetic Confession too, refuse to be content with completely free calling by the Spirit or with "democratic church government" in the literal sense. They declare that the ordination of presbyters by presbyters (amongst whom the *pastors* hold supreme responsibility in the manner of the early Christian bishops) is the apostolic form of Church order. See J. Pannier: *Calvin et l'Épiscopat* in: *Rev. d'Hist. et de Philos. relig.* VI, 305 ff.; W. Niesel: *Bekenntnisschriften u. Kirchenordnungen d. ref. Kirche* (²1945)76, 255; H. Heppe – E. Bizer: *Reformed Dogmatics* (London 1950) Chap. 27, *On the Church,* p. 657 ff.; K. Barth: *The Doctrine of the Word of God* (Edinburgh 1936) p. 106 ff.

Lutheran church: "No one will suppose that one of the apostles would recognize again in this formula the *ecclesia* of which he had living experience."[211] We do not want to adopt this verdict without recalling the efforts of the German Protestant authors of the "Augsburg Confession" to retain bishops "by divine right", provided they are "lawful bishops", exercising their powers in the spirit of the gospel.[212]

The basic intention of this is in line with ancient Catholic tradition and is clearly much nearer to the apostolic norm than is a mere fraternal fellowship with the denial of all "institutionalism" in Brunner's sense.

[211] *Ibid.* 103.

[212] J. T. Müller: *Die symbol. Bücher d. ev.-luth. Kirche* ([10]1907): *Confession of Augsburg* 14, 28; *Apol.* 13, 7–13 14 28. Of endeavours to resolve the "state of emergency", W. Stählin writes: "Because in the end the appointed incumbents and leaders in the spiritual office, the bishops that is, refused to carry out the work of renewing the Church, Luther saw no other way but to link ecclesiastical office with the congregation, with the priesthood of all Christians. Against the obvious objection, which naturally troubled him greatly, that the congregation are in no position to test Christian doctrine . . . to depose unorthodox preachers, Luther found comfort in a notion from the social teaching of his age which affirmed that the rights of each corporate body are proportionate to its best members. Luther himself, indeed, sought more and more as time went on to join the ministry fundamentally to an authority which was separated from the congregation. What makes sense in an emergency and may be practicable in extraordinary circumstances, is bound to disrupt not only ecclesiastical authority but the Christian community as well, when it is expressed as a theological principle" (*Vom göttlichen Geheimnis* 1936, 101). The *Confession of Augsburg* upholds the ancient "Church order and the gradation" within the holy ministry (Art. 14). The fifth article with its discrepancies between the Latin and the German texts betrays the fact that "the fatal limitation of the ministry in the Church to the office of preaching had not yet been settled" (Stählin: *op. cit.* 102).

Cullmann is in error when he says that the New Testament contains "nothing" concerning the manner and form in which authority is handed on. The imposition of hands of the apostolic or post-apostolic bearers of authority is no mere external act which men in the Church might use at their discretion. "The New Testament understands the imposition of hands as more than a rite and symbol."[213] According to the Scripture it is the sign of the conferring of authority in the Holy Spirit – presupposing a corresponding disposition of faith, and devotion to the service of the people. The author of the Acts of the Apostles "obviously makes a point of tracing the various ecclesiastical offices of his own time back to their origins, . . . clearly he lays much store by a regular, solemn introduction to office. The acceptance of an ecclesiastical ministry involved an ordination."[214] Judging from the Pastoral Epistles,[215] it is "undoubtedly correct to describe ordination as a sacramental act".[216] This, of course, does not imply an "automatic guarantee against corruption", or that it is performed according to a "self-subsistent sacred law", but rather that the recipient accepts the authority as well as the sacred responsibility of ruling in the Spirit of Christ and in no other way, "as a servant and steward of the mysteries of God".[217] But as, the imposition of hands represents the apostolic form of passing on authority and is a tradition

---

[213] E. Sommerlath in Zoellner-Stählin: *op. cit.* 162. Cf. the *Confession of Augsburg* Art. 13, 7–12 (in J. T. Müller: *op. cit.* 203) where sacramental imposition of hands is recognized – in a section containing polemic against popular Catholic conceptions of the "sacrificing priesthood".

[214] H. v. Campenhausen: *Kirchl. Amt* 168. Acts 6:1ff.; 13:2f.; 14:23.

[215] 2 Tim. 1:6; 1 Tim. 4:16.

[216] H. v. Campenhausen: *op. cit.* 126 and what follows at 128.

[217] 1 Cor. 13:1.

reaching back to the New Testament, *in possessione,* that is by apostolic institution, the alleged theological possibility of departing from that to "another form" would have to be rigorously proved, and indeed from Scripture or early apostolic tradition. Otherwise it can only be regarded as a deviation from recognized Christian principles.

The assurance with which E. Brunner speaks is astonishing when he says that in the New Testament "*cheirotonia* has nothing whatever to do with the laying on of hands"; and that not imposition of hands but raising of hands is the customary manner of voting for those to be ordained, and that "nowhere do we see the laying on of hands in connection "with the transference of a special function or office".[218] It is true that imposition of hands is not always the sign of ordination to office: it can mediate healing power to the sick,[219] or the fulness of the Holy Spirit's gifts to the baptized;[220] but, apart from the Pastoral Epistles, which are after all still part of the New Testament, there remains Acts 14:23, the passage to which Brunner alludes. When Paul and Barnabas "appointed elders for them in each congregation by imposition of hands *(cheirotonia)*" this rite might indeed signify the raising of hands by electors as well, but in this case that would not make sense, for only two apostles are involved. The phrase is literally "extending of hands" and as such comes very close to imposition of hands in the purely external sense. Translating more freely, however, we may say: "they appointed elders on their behalf" or "they installed elders for them".[221] Since this obviously

[218] Emil Brunner: *op. cit.* p. 80.
[219] Mark 5:23; Luke 5:13.   [220] Acts 8:17.
[221] Thus A. Wikenhauser. *Die Apg.* ([2]1957) 135.

refers to appointments to ecclesiastical ministry and responsibility, we have Acts 6:6 to tell us how the Seven were appointed to assist the apostles: "they (the apostles) praying, imposed hands upon them." And so – *pace* E. Brunner – there was imposition of hands in order to effect the "passing on of a special ministry or office". The Pastoral Epistles only corroborate this.

Taking everything into consideration, it cannot be considered an innovation when Clement of Rome, referring to the existing "apostolic succession" – and not to justify one about to be created, writes to the Corinthians: "The apostles preached to us the Gospel received from Jesus Christ and Jesus Christ was God's Ambassador . . . . From land to land, accordingly, and from city to city they preached, and from among their earliest converts appointed men whom they tested by the Spirit, to act as bishops and deacons for the future believers . . . . Our apostles were also given to understand by our Lord Jesus Christ that the office of the bishop would give rise to intrigues. For this reason, equipped as they were with perfect foreknowledge, they appointed the men mentioned before, and afterwards laid down a rule once for all to this effect: when men die, other approved men shall succeed to their sacred ministery."[222]

In this passage Clement is obviously referring to those "earliest converts" mentioned by St. Paul in 1 Corinthians 16:15 ff. as leading the congregations; and if he is convinced that the apostles founded their regulation of the congregations with an eye to future difficulties, then "the same assumption is made by

[222] Clement of Rome: *Epistle to the Corinthians* 42 44; *Ancient Christian Writers* (1946) London, Vol 1. I. p. 36.

Luke in Acts 20:29", followed by 2 Timothy 3:1 ff., 2 Peter 3:3 and Jude 17 f. who "drew attention to this even more insistently".[223]

All things go to show that the content of the theological technical expression "apostolic succession" may be taken as a biblical and early Christian reality.

Cullmann, however, affirms that Scripture alludes to a different (or at least to *yet another*) form of passing on of authority. The "only New Testament text" which speaks explicitly of this transition from the apostles to the post-apostolic period, and of the post-apostolic "chain", is said to be a sentence in the Sacerdotal Prayer when Jesus prays for his apostles "and for them also who through their word shall believe in me".[224] The word through which they believe is said to be "the Apostolic writings" and the uniqueness of the apostolic office he regards as corresponding in later times to the unique work of the apostles embodied in the Scriptures. ". . . the apostles are followed by the entire Church of the believers."[225]

Cullmann's comparison, however, is invalid. It is not the apostles and faithful who are contrasted – the apostles themselves are numbered amongst the faithful – but the apostles who came to believe through Jesus' own word, and those who came to believe through the word of the apostles. "Word" is used obviously, as it often is, in a comprehensive sense. The whole of life along with the proclamation of the faith is the word which arouses belief. Holy Scripture is not mentioned – unless it be the Old Testament to which reference is made. The

---

[223] H. v. Campenhausen: *Kirchl. Amt* 99.
[224] John 17:20. [225] Cullmann: *Peter* pp. 224–6.

apostles found faith by "hearing the word" or, we may say, by being with the Lord. The others find faith "by hearing" and hearing pre-supposes "preachers" and preaching, a "being sent".[226] It is true that the word of the apostles will one day find its way into Scripture to become the basis of later preaching, its "ultimate foundation" as Pius XII has said;[227] but proclaiming the faith will for ever remain essential "that they may believe", for Christianity is not a book-religion nor the Church an institution for literate members only.

Or is it that the unique and non-recurrent character of the apostolic office is respected precisely because what continues is not the apostolate of the Twelve and the Petrine primacy, but "the embodiment of their persons and work, that is the apostolic Scriptures"?[228] We have no wish to draw Cullmann into self-contradiction. According to him, apostolic succession has to do with the continuance of the authority of leadership, from the apostles onwards. On the other hand there appear in addition, not all at once but gradually, the Scriptures of the New Testament. These originated in the apostolic age, were collected, defined and given canonical status in the course of three centuries. They appear as an embodiment or reflection of the work of the apostles and now become the basis of all preaching, through which "the historically unique effect of their persons and their work continues to exist ... ." Does that mean, as is often said – in all good faith no doubt –, that the

---

[226] Rom. 10:14.

[227] Pius XII: *Munificentissimus Deus*. Cf. Card. Aug. Bea in: *Civiltà catt.* December 2, 1950.

[228] *Peter* p. 225: "This is only possible ..." and also p. 226: "When we read the Gospels ..."

"authentic" or "valid" apostolic succession consists in the agreement of the Church with the preaching of the apostles, with the apostolic word of Scripture, so that the office of succession becomes superfluous? If that were true, this would first imply departing from Scripture and the apostolic Church, for both testify to the derivation of an authority of leadership from the apostles; and second, in practice, as experience shows, we would be left with only the idea of or the desire for Church unity, with neither unity of belief nor of prayer, neither unity of preaching nor of public worship and the sacraments. In short, unity as Jesus and the apostles thought of it would be made illusory by such a theology of "Scripture alone" – so that the theological principle condemns itself.

It is not as though the lawful legitimation of "institution" in the ranks of those who held authority were intrinsically or primarily the link between the early Church, the apostles, including Peter, and the later Church with its spiritual shepherds, including Peter II. Their unity is primarily "the unity of their testimony to Christ and their calling" in the Holy Spirit;[229] but because "we and the Holy Spirit have decided"[230] what the Lord demands of the Church in a particular situation, and because the Spirit as a "helper" will make known, to those who humbly supplicate, what is to come, and will recall to their minds the revelation of Christ,[231] therefore the spiritual shepherds follow one another as "bearers of the same unchanging commission";[232] and consequently, shepherds and flock are

[229] H. v. Campenhausen: *Kirchl. Amt* 31.
[230] Acts 15:28.   [231] John 14:16, 26; 16:13.
[232] H. v. Campenhausen: *Kirchl. Amt* 169 327. Cf. R. Baumann: *Des Petrus Bekenntnis und Schlüssel* (1950) 17.

so dependent upon each other for the sake of Christ that belief in the promise of the Holy Spirit to those so united is inseparable from belief in Christ himself.

In Cullmann, therefore, I do not find any "supersession" of the apostolic office, more precisely, of the authority of leadership in the Church through the Holy Spirit with the sign of imposition of hands, although I do find it in other writers. There can certainly be no question of an authority of leadership passing on merely through the work of the apostles perpetuated in Scripture. Why is this impossible? Because no matter how much the Spirit works through the Scriptures within the congregation or in individuals a community which says the Lord's Prayer may well exist without Scripture, and even without human officials. But a community which baptizes may exist without the Scriptures but not without human officials authorized to effect admittance. A community which celebrates the Lord's Supper may exist without Scriptures but not without someone to preside at the liturgy – the *pater familias* who breaks the bread or the "elders" who are responsible for upholding the principle: "holy things to holy people". In order to carry out both baptism and Eucharist in due form, the Scriptures are certainly not required. Paul derived these things from a living tradition and it was by living tradition that they were handed on further. In other words: the very innermost life of the Church, in distinction from preaching the word, has the very slightest dependence upon the availability of the New Testament Scriptures. So little is religion, faith, Christ, the heart of the Church, locked within a book.

For all time, the Scriptures are the basis of the proclamation of the faith – more precisely: the basis is the revelation of

Christ according to the testimony of early apostolic tradition and the Scriptures. Holy Scripture is first and foremost the book of those who proclaim the faith because not all can read, nor personally possess the Scriptures.[233] On this point we gladly quote Emil Brunner. We receive the testimony of Christ through the Church. "The community of believers itself, however, does not live first of all on the Bible – the Christian religion is not the religion of a book – but on the living word of our contemporaries who can testify to us themselves that Christ is the living and present Lord."[234] Those who spread the living word are many but these many, along with their congregations, are to form the holy unity in the spirit of love, that "perfect unity" of the Church of Christ (John 17:23). In her essence, the Church is "love",[235] love imparted through the Holy Spirit. The Spirit is the spirit of unity,[236] and the "sacrament of the Church", the Eucharistic meal, is fellowship with Christ and fellowship of his members with one another, so that they are as closely united as the members of a body. If the body is made up of men, the body of Christ is thus visible, no matter how invisible the mystical interior, which is the grace of the Spirit. Visible unity, however, means that all are arranged in an orderly unity – *homologias tēn gnosin* ("knowledge of love-inspired unity"), *syntaxin epechein* ("to perceive the

---

[233] On the use of Scripture in the second century see J. Jeremias in: *Th. Bl.* 1936, 43 f.

[234] E. Brunner: *The Christian Doctrine of God* (*Dogmatics* Vol. I, London 1949) p. 19.

[235] Ignatius of Antioch: *Romans* 1. Cf. O. Perler in: *Divus Thomas* 1944, 413 ff.

[236] 1 Cor. 12; Eph. 4:3.

bond"), is how the fathers of the Council of Chalcedon describe it in their letter to Leo I.[237] This does not denote dominion over slaves, but responsible leadership corresponding to a willingness to be led. If this is basically lacking, then an essential feature of the apostolic Church is lacking, an essential feature not merely of her structure, of the visible form of the Church, but of her soul as well. For if this is lacking there is no longer any place for proving that brotherly unity which, in the apostolic Church as in the Pauline-charismatic Church, is founded upon "obedience" to the apostles,[238] that is to the presidents descended from the apostles,[239] upon obedience for Christ's sake and from love.[240] This concerns not something foreign to love, but the proving of love.[241]

Or does obedience to men in the name of Christ become obedience to the word of Scripture in the name of Christ? What a person reads can be interpreted according to his own feelings. It is so easy, it is so human to find in the written word the path one desires to follow.[242] Primitive Christian obedience is more than obedience to the Scriptures – which were only in the process of becoming –, more, even, than obedience to the congregation; for if it is the collective community and not responsible pastors we have in mind, then it is certainly not obedience we are talking about, but only reverence, respect, piety. Obedience and subjection to men are biblical, even Pauline concepts – but everything stands beneath the sign of

[237] Denzinger: *Ench.* n. 149.   [238] 2 Cor. 2:9; 2 Thess. 3:14.
[239] 1 Thess. 5:12; Heb. 13:17.
[240] Cf. Luke 10:16.   [241] Cf. John 14:21.
[242] J. H. Newman: *Discourses addressed to Mixed Congregations* (London 1849) X p. 203.

love, and has, therefore, a religious meaning. In this very way St. Paul sees the Church: 1 Corinthians 12 deals with the Church as a body, 1 Corinthians 13 with the Church as love, 1 Corinthians 14 with the Church as the order of love. The three chapters all belong together.[243]

Is the Christian sacrificing thereby what is holy, or, is he not, on the contrary thus realizing holiness? Ecclesiastical obedience extends as far as the Church speaks in Christ's name in the service of the kingdom of God according to the meaning of Scripture, and is the foundation of all the Church's activity. Only if, in a concrete instance of the exercise of ecclesiastical authority, the opposite is clearly proved to be true, as in the case of Joan of Arc, does the love we owe consist not in obedience to men in place of God, but in obedience to God instead of outward human obedience.[244]

5. The Petrine succession

a. Bible and Apostolic Church as sources

The Petrine succession is the accentuated line in the apostolic succession. A consideration of the text of Matthew 16:17ff. will perhaps help to show whether it is in harmony with the spirit of Scripture.

It is true that the Lord gave the power, designated as "binding and loosing" to the other apostles as well,[245] corresponding

---

[243] Following a lecture by H. U. v. Balthasar.
[244] Acts 4:19; 5:29 Cf. Thomas Aquinas: *De veritate,* qu. 17, 3–5.
[245] Matt. 18:18.

to the authority given them on their first mission to preach the kingdom of God, for the peace of some, to the judgment of others.[246]

In John 20:23 also, the apostles receive authority corresponding to that of Matthew 18:18. But he gave it first to Peter. The first word was addressed to "one". In this way he was providing that the Church should be the instrument of the kingdom of God as a "unity"; and it is only against that background that the chosen disciples are given any sort of authority at all, with leadership through an authority of final appeal. All this is to assure the unity and the enduring existence of the Church as the instrument of the kingdom of God. How can a state, or a city, or a household endure if it is divided against itself?[247]

It is true that Peter's rank as the one who acknowledged the Messiah, and his status as first apostle and rock-foundation of the Church is non-recurring. There is no question of inheritance of these things or of any replacement of the one apostolic beginning appointed by Christ. The foundation-stone has been laid once and for all; but just as with the apostles, so with the first apostle it is true that this unique, non-recurrent characteristic includes something which lasts for ever. Peter's rôle as a witness of the revelation is unique: his rôle as the exponent of unity and the one who is authorized to look after this unity is perpetual.

Jesus built his church upon Peter as rock-bottom or foundation-stone. As we have said, it is no material building, but a spiritual one made up of living men animated by a spirit. Peter himself as foundation is the most important of these "living stones".[248] Individual men come and go: the structure of the

---

[246] Matt. 10:5ff.   [247] Matt. 12:25.   [248] 1 Pet. 2:5.

building remains. The continuance of the building does not rest upon the material identity of the stones – they are "living" stones, men who make up the church. The continuity of the Church is guaranteed by the enduring presence of Christ who inspires the whole temple and the individual members alike.[249] This is the continuity of the mystical "body" in Paul's image, whose cells – men – change, but whose formal principle and structure remain – if it is to be the same church.

Against the church founded upon Peter, or, as we may interpret the text, against Peter "hell" will launch its attack, but it will not prevail. Peter, the rock whom Jesus supported with his will, his promise, his intercession, dies. He is no longer present; but hell continues. Or could we say that, in the absence of a living foundation-stone to support the living stones of future generations, a dead rock, a distant memory would suffice to halt the advance of the powers of darkness, or to strengthen the brethren? Would the church in the year 200 or 2000 be strengthened by the fact that there had once been a Peter who received a promise for himself personally? Would the church continue in the Holy Spirit because the Spirit was once poured out upon the church led by Peter? The work of the powers of darkness in the year 200 or 2000 would be all the easier in regard to some "historical rock", a commemorative "Chair of Peter", the more devoutly the pious venerated the memorial plinth.

And consider this point: Peter was not installed there and then, but set apart in advance for the function of being rock and bearer of the keys. The church was not yet in existence, unless in embryo as *Ecclesia designata*. Peter is not yet the "key-bearer" or "shepherd

---

[249] John 16:13ff.; 1 Cor. 13:16; 12:13ff.; Eph. 2:22.

of the lambs and sheep". The Lord himself is still present and, as yet, requires no representative, no other in a commissioned function as a rock or shepherd supported by himself. Soon, however, such a one will step forward. The very next verse speaks of this future occasion.[250] Peter is appointed for this time after Jesus has gone home from this earth. The idea of a succession is contained in Jesus' own perspective. It is true that Jesus has no successor in his own unique dignity as "the great Shepherd of the sheep",[251] and as "bearer of the keys of death and of hell";[252] but for the period of time when he will not be visibly present, the disciples are to be able to cling to one who represents him, and Jesus will "strengthen" him. And when Peter shall be there no longer, what then? Is this thought quite outside Jesus' range of vision, or even contrary to his thought?

Let us consider further. At Caesarea Philippi, or on that last evening when he prayed for Peter, or at the Lake of Gennesareth after Easter when he committed the "sheep and the lambs" to him to tend, was Jesus thinking solely of Peter himself or of the church of the future? There can be no doubt that he had the church in mind. His own words imply this, for he spoke of "my church". He is concerned with the affairs of God in the future, for he knows that soon he will be taken away. It is only on this account, for the sake of the kingdom of God that he speaks to Peter, and not because of any personal liking or even because of his sublime confession of faith, although the latter may have provided him with a suitable occasion for making the promise. He was thinking of the future, was making provision for his church. In Spirit he saw the powers of darkness

---

[250] Matt. 16:21ff. [251] Heb. 16:13. [252] Apoc. 1:18. Cf. 3:7.

94

at work, ready to make an assault upon the church; and as long as the assault lasted, the living rock of resistance must be there – a living rock, not the memory of one long dead.

Peter, on making his confession of faith, received the keys. The church's confession is inaugurated. "Confession of faith and the keys endure throughout the same length of time."[253] If the confession is to continue, so must the function indicated by the keys of Peter. The rabbis had a telling symbol for the passing on of the authority of leadership. They hung a band or chain with a key round the new incumbent. Jesus commissioned Peter so that his office of key-bearer should be "the model of all office and ministry in the church".[254] In a certain sense, everyone who shares in Christ through baptism and faith, shares also in his office of priest, king, and prophet. To serve God is to rule, to intercede is to act as a priest, to bear witness is to speak with the voice of a prophet. Peter, however, received the keys as the one standing for the whole church and as the first to be responsible for its unity; for the keys signify the fulness of sharing in Christ's authority. Did he receive the authority only as a personal gift or as the first in the line of bearers of keys? The apostles' powers to lead the church continued on – as we have seen. Surely, the first of these powers too must continue, the powers of him who received the keys. Or, keeping the same metaphor, are we to assume that the keys were, as it were, buried with Peter? No doubt seems possible to us in the meaning of Jesus.

For the ancient people of God, whose traditions Jesus took up, the departing Moses had appointed Josue to be his successor.

[253] R. Baumann: *Des Petrus Bekenntnis und Schlüssel* (1950) 23.
[254] E. Stauffer: *op. cit.* 16.

The scribes sat upon "Moses' *cathedra*", and the high-priest as president of the great council ruled as the final court of appeal in religious matters over the Jews of the diaspora also. In short, what had been unique in Moses' mission did not make succession impossible. As we have seen, even the Ebionites, that Jewish-Christian sect who stemmed from the Jerusalem church, saw the matter in this light. They merely proposed a different person as the first link in the chain of succession; but they too, had a chain of succession – so much was the principle of succession in supreme church leadership taken for granted in the earliest period. They claimed the primacy for James and his successors, because only in this way, they believed, could Jewish interests be assured against Gentile-Christian predominance. As Cullmann observes, [255] James was for them the "leader of the holy church of the Hebrews and of the churches founded everywhere by God's providence";[256] and "he or the one who happened to be his successor at the time" was held responsible for purity of doctrine.[257]

Against the Clementine back-dating of the "monarchical episcopate" in the apostolic period H. v. Campenhausen[258] argues that precisely on Palestinian soil it was a question of "handing on a doctrine" guaranteed through the *cathedra,* and that the bishop was surrounded by the council of "elders". But that the normative tradition of doctrine was regarded as linked with the *cathedra* of a primus is testified both for the Jewish-Christians represented by the *Pseudo-Clementina*[259] and

[255] *Peter* p. 230.   [256] Ps.-Clement: *Epistle of Clement to James.*
[257] *Recogn.* 4, 35.
[258] H. v. Campenhausen in: *Zts f. Kirchengeschichte* 1950–1, 143 f.
[259] *Hom.* 18, 7.

for the Western order.[260] It certainly corresponds to the church order of the Bible, as attested for the time of the apostles by the gospels. The "bishop of bishops", like his colleagues, may well be no absolute "monarch" ruling in the style of an early emperor or caliph. On all important issues he acts in consultation with his co-apostles and the congregation, as the Acts of the Apostles testifies.[261] Even the "monarchical bishop" – Ignatius of Antioch – is surrounded by his presbyters, as earlier, Clement of Rome acts in union with the community, but ultimately there is one who "feeds the sheep and the lambs", while the others "lead the portion of the flock entrusted to you".[262]

At this point we may be allowed a slight digression. Keeping within the field of early Christian thought, we can find a concrete example of what has been said in the person of Cyprian. He is indeed no pliable witness, no devotee of absolute Petrine rule, attests no "papalism" – as Soloviev said[263] – but rather the organic interrelation of the college of bishops and the primus, with all the tensions, as they already appear in the circle of the apostles, resolved and ever to be resolved anew by love. He is able to write: "No doubt the others were all that Peter was but a primacy is given to Peter, and it is (thus) made clear that there is but one Church and one Chair."[264] For Cyprian, the Petrine office is *radix et matrix Ecclesiae catholicae*, root and womb of the Catholic

---

[260] Clement of Rome: *To the Corinthians* 44; Ignatius of Antioch: *Romans* 1.
[261] See note on Acts 6:6 in Karrer's edition of N. T.
[262] 1 Pet. 5:3. [263] *Irénikon* 1926, 78.
[264] Cyprian: *De unit.* 4. *Ancient Christian Writers* (1957) Longmans Green, Vol. XXV. p. 46.

Church.[265] The unity of the church has the foundation of its existence in the Petrine office.[266] Cyprian distinguishes between a "personal investiture of Peter" as the historical origin of church unity, and the perpetual primacy as the foundation of unity in the enduring church. For him the promise in Matthew 16 is certainly "the foundation-document of the one church with a single episcopate which extends down the centuries from Peter; and the power which holds the church together, both spiritually and externally, flows from Christian love"[267] – but "in Peter" the unity is represented and guaranteed. And even if Cyprian may be a bit uneasy about an active manifestation of central church leadership, for him the characteristic thing, the enduring *raison d'être* of unity is the duty which the bishops have of joint reference, in the spirit of love, to the one centre, to the "chief church" with its leading apostolic chair, to the *apostolicae Cathedrae principatus*.[268]

If the church of apostolic times, although a fellowship of brethren bound in the Spirit of love, is at the same time characterized

---

[265] Cyprian: *Ep.* 48, 3.

[266] See K. Adam: *Ges. Aufs.* (1936) 150 ff. (discussing E. Caspar: *Primatus Petri* [1927]).

[267] H. Koch: *Cathedra Petri* (1930) 164.

[268] Cyprian: *Ep.* 59, 14; 43, 3, 7. Cyprian's *"Ecclesia principalis"* (chief church) is probably influenced by Irenaeus' "potentior principalis" (III 3, 2). The moral obligation of unity with the contemporary successor to Peter is mentioned in this letter and in his principal work also. He was much concerned to support Pope Cornelius against Novatian. Cf. E. Caspar: *op. cit.* 304 ff.; K. Adam: *op. cit.*; P. Batiffol: *Cath. Petri* (1938); O. Perler: *Röm. Quartalschr.* 1936, 1 ff., 151 ff. As Cullmann says (*Peter* p. 167 n. 14) "Cyprian's exposition could scarcely be regarded as *entirely* consistent and unified". See B. Altaner: *Patrology* Herder-Nelson, London, and Herder and Herder, New York 1960, p. 193 f.

by a "holy order" – "hierarchy" in the original meaning of the word –, by a collegiate leadership in the same Holy Spirit; if this circle of authorized officials is given a primus who carries the keys and is a supreme shepherd of the "lambs and the sheep"; and if all of this has been provided by the Lord of the church for the sake of the kingdom of God, so that the church, as God's special people, may be the instrument for inaugurating the kingdom of God, how then could the apostles have come to think that later on the church would no longer require the same order and structure, that they could change over, as they felt inclined, to some other structure, no longer having to be both charismatic and hierarchical, and yet, with its new form, still the same church as Christ conceived it, – arguing that it is, after all, a question of the inner Spirit and not of outward form? Why then did he himself give it this form?

The church in the early centuries, the apostolic and subapostolic church, believed itself bound to this form, in the East as in the West. From time to time, new links were added to the chain by the imposition of hands of the former pastors, along with a certain co-operation of the people. The consecratory sacrament of baptism which conferred membership in the body of Christ corresponds to the consecratory sacrament of imposition of hands which initiated into the ministry within the church. In the former the consecration is effected by "water and Spirit", in the latter by "imposition of hands and Spirit". The consecration of the general priesthood corresponds to ordination of the bearers of authority. The Lord himself has ordained that the holy order of love will never lack "one to preside", as Ignatius of Antioch said, that at no time the house will lack one who carries the keys, that in place of Peter there will always be one to exercise the responsibility of supreme pastor, therefore no man may ever depart from this arrangement, if the structure which Christ gave his church is to remain.

On the other hand, the limitation to a specific community or place – a view which Cullmann ascribes to Catholic dogmatics[269] – is a matter outside dogmatic theology, that is to say, it requires more exact distinctions and explanations in order justly to represent the view of Catholic theology. Cullmann says: "If we wish to derive further from the saying that after Peter also there must be in the Church a universal leadership that administers the keys, the binding and loosing, this cannot take place in the sense of a limitation to the future occupants of one episcopal see;"[270] and again: "Developments of the post-apostolic period of church history, important as they may be ... cannot give an exclusively normative position to any of those leading places."[271] To begin with, no divine right is derived from the post-apostolic rôle of the Roman see. First, it is correct that the notion of primacy in itself does not contain a link with one particular congregation or place. Peter was completely free to shift his residence from Jerusalem to Antioch or Rome or wherever he liked. Wherever he was he was the key-bearer, just as wherever there are believers, there is the spiritual "house". Secondly, it is correct that Peter's final residence in Rome is the "decisive argument" for the historical primacy of the Roman episcopal see within the church at large.[272] When Peter, apparently after some hesitation as to the expediency of the move, and certainly not immediately after his flight from Jerusalem, turned to Rome as his primatial see, Catholic theology from then on regards the primacy as tied to the Ro-

[269] *Peter* p. 236 ff.   [270] *Ibid.* 242.
[271] *Ibid.* 240 f.   [272] *Ibid.* 237.

man episcopal see. This view is put forward today by general consent, although there is no binding dogma on the subject, and the view does not imply that the Pope at any particular time must necessarily be in Rome or that the city of Rome or the Christian community there is assured of a perpetual existence. *Roma aeterna* is a pre-Christian imperial title, and Christ made no promise either to a particular nation or to a particular city, but only to the church and her leadership, and with the promise gave divine right and a divine obligation to the church that the new primates amongst those in authority correspond to him who was first amongst those to whom Christ gave authority.

b. How to explain the historical translation from Jerusalem to Rome

K. Holl[273] develops a theory which is interesting in many respects. We recognize in him the inspiration behind Emil Brunner's "charismatic-Pauline" notion of the Church – Brunner, however, is much more radical than K. Holl –, and also behind Cullmann's notion about the primitive Church "under James". We need not go back over these two theories. K. Holl, the expert in church history, has gone into the matter of the historical translation of the primacy from Jerusalem to Rome.

Holl's view is roughly this. The primitive church was a single large congregation, and freshly founded congregations were regarded as mere offshoots from the mother church. Jerusalem was the first, James was its bishop, assisted by other "pillars". The Pauline congregations form a contrast to this. Although, from the original congregation, Paul "took over the concept of the

---

[273] K. Holl: *Gesammelte Aufs.* II (1928) 56, 61–5.

church as an institution, and although he recognized the office of the Twelve as the first apostles to be called", nonetheless the Pauline congregations represent something "new". 1. "The living Christ" is their head. 2. "The apostles" are only messengers, instruments of Christ. 3. "Each Christian", in Paul's eyes, "has the right to regard everything, even Paul and Peter, as subject to himself." Holl quotes 1 Corinthians 3:21 f. in support of this, Brunner, 1 Corinthians 2:15. 4. Paul does not concede any pride of place to Jerusalem. He would not have its association with the "saints" who live there severed, but the other congregations, too, are holy. This means that here "the primacy is disputed for the first time" – the primacy of particular persons and of a particular place; and Paul has "severed the connection with the place", has "won his case as far as Jerusalem is concerned".

External development came to his aid – the death of James, the destruction of Jerusalem and the increase in the number of Gentile-Christian congregations as Christianity spread. By destroying the primacy of Jerusalem Paul "prepared the way for the other primacy – that of Rome". "The Roman papacy is nothing but the re-erection of the position of James." "The Roman congregation knew how to make use of the accident that Peter and Paul suffered martyrdom there ... Rome becomes Jerusalem."

Apart from the James-legend, the historical sketch of the transference is excellent, and we may well agree that in the end it "was not just chance that Jerusalem was destroyed and Peter and Paul were martyred in that place where all the peoples of the world then converged".[274] Indeed, the struc-

[274] R. Baumann: *Des Petrus Bekenntnis und Schlüssel* (1950) 138.

ture of the Acts of the Apostles makes it plain that the development of the church was pointing to Rome as the chief congregation. It was to Rome that Paul wrote the letter with a concluding greeting, such as he uses for no other church: "All the churches of Christ salute you."[275]

It is very likely that 1 Peter was written between 61 and 64 from Rome – "Babylon". All the other early church statements become clear and easily understood if we make the obvious assumption that Peter and Paul lived in Rome and died there as martyrs. "Any other presumption can never cite even a single document in its positive support."[276]

Certainly there was nothing in the idea of the church or of the primacy which logically compelled Peter to turn to Rome; and for this reason, as far as succession in the Petrine office is concerned, neither was "one particular church" determined once and for all from the start.[277] Nor does the theological truth of the supreme pastoral office in the church depend upon the maximum historical probability of Peter's sojourn in Rome, nor is that the starting-point for any strictly held "eternal truth of faith" that the *Cathedra Petri* is joined to the Roman episcopal see. Cullmann, it is true, cites a series of Catholic theologians[278] who, he thinks, represent this "more liberal" view: Stan. Dunin Borkowski, R. Graber, L. Kösters, Ch. Journet; but he considers that they contradict the "wording of the Vatican pronouncement" which speaks of "the holy Roman see, which was founded by Peter and consecrated by his blood".

[275] Rom. 16:16.
[276] H. Lietzmann: *Petrus und Paulus in Rom* (1915) 171.
[277] *Peter* p. 231 f.
[278] *Ibid.* p. 236.

There is, however, no contradiction between the said theologians and the Vatican Council. We have to distinguish the question whether the primacy of the Roman bishop depends upon Peter's historic residence in and episcopacy of Rome, from the other question whether the primacy is for ever tied to the Roman see. The theologians mentioned have grounds for denying the first proposition while accepting the second as theologically founded, but not as an article of faith.

The fathers of the Vatican Council, in the statement quoted, accept the sojourn and martyrdom of Peter in Rome as an historical fact, but do not propose this as an article of faith. The definitions of the Vatican Council, like other definitions, deal exclusively with revelation, and, according to the explanations of the conciliar theologians, are always contained in the canon; and concerning this second chapter, the canon runs: "Therefore if anyone says that it is not according to the institution of Christ our Lord himself, that is, by divine law, that St. Peter has perpetual successors in the primacy over the whole church; or if anyone says that the Roman Pontiff is not the successor of St. Peter in the same primacy, let him be anathema."[279]

The continuous connection of the primacy to the Roman see is affirmed generally by modern Catholic theologians. Th. Granderath, editor and exponent of the Vatican proceedings, expressed himself with reserve.[280] None, however, proposes this view as an article of faith. As appears from the Acts of the Vatican Council, the fathers of the council did not wish to decide "whether the primacy and the dignity of the Roman episcopate were

[279] Vat. Council IV, 2 (Denzinger: *Ench.* n. 1824) text in *The Church Teaches* 1955 B. Herder Book Co. 97.
[280] Granderath: *Gesch. d. Vat. Konzils* III (1960) 482f.

indissolubly linked". There were long deliberations on the subject, three different opinions were considered and it was agreed "not to incline too much to any of them".[281] The most recent relevant study, the *Theologia fundamentalis* of the Spanish Jesuits M. Nicolau and J. Salaverri,[282] argues: "The proof which we advance of the primacy of the Roman supreme pastor is completely independent both from the fact of St. Peter's stay in Rome, and from the right by which Peter united the primacy with the Roman episcopal office." This style of proof of the succession *per se* is said to have been employed by Cardinal Bellarmine and to have gained adherents, so that even the fathers of the council, appealing to Bellarmine, repeatedly stressed, "that the question about succession in the primacy is independent of Peter's having been bishop of Rome, and of his right – whether divine or human and ecclesiastical – to have occupied that see".

In terms of this argument, one might posit that Peter, without ever having been in Rome and exercising any function in the church there, had in some way or other arranged that the Roman bishop became his successor in the primacy – in some such way as Moses appointed Josue his successor. In this way it is presupposed that the link between the Roman bishopric and the primacy could only be constructed by Peter himself – and was constructed –, and that accordingly, this link can be broken – if not as a concept, at least with reference to the place – only by Peter's successor, unless it be that during a possible conjunction of a vacancy in the see with a state of emergency, the most competent authorities in the church decide the matter.

For the faithful, the practical consideration is simple: because

[281] Granderath: *op. cit.* 305.
[282] 2nd edition, Madrid 1952, n. 428, p. 631.

it is based upon Christ's promise for his church that there will always be a supreme leadership, and because, on the other hand, none other than the bishop of Rome has laid claim to this leadership and had his claim recognized by the church, therefore I know that the bishops of Rome are the successors of Peter even before I have been convinced by historical proof that Peter lived and was martyred in Rome. In fact there is as great certainty about these historical facts as there is about any other well accredited facts of history we like to mention.

It is possible for us to imagine, more or less, what the considerations were which once led the itinerant Peter to turn his steps towards Rome. Let us start from later analogies which allow us to project certain conclusions back into the apostolic age. In his farewell to Constantinople in 381, Gregory Nazianzen, the Patriarch, praises the rôle of his city. It is "the eye, the bond between land and sea, the place to which people stream in from the ends of the earth to take away provisions from the common store of faith".[283] The bishops of Gaul write to Leo I that they had fixed on Arles as metropolis of their country, because there, "the people from all the provincial towns assemble for many practical purposes".[284] True, these are analogies from a later period, but if, in 58, Paul turned his eyes from Jerusalem to Rome from similar considerations,[285] and even earlier in Corinth had "often purposed" to travel to Rome,[286] then the most obvious course of all to follow, for him who knew that he was the "fisher of men"[287] and had, by divine impulse, opened the door to the Gentiles,[288] was to make his goal the capital city of the whole

[283] Gregory Nazianzen. Sermon 42, 10.
[284] Migne *PL* 4, 882. [285] Acts 23:11.
[286] Rom. 1:13. [287] Luke 5:2 [288] Acts 10–11.

world. Whether, following some theologians, we posit a special divine inspiration for this, or, with others, simply put it down to considerations of expediency in the service of the kingdom of God,[289] the result is the same in the end: vision was directed towards the further development of the church.

Already the Jewish-Christians had moved from the centre of development to the fringe. The best amongst them aided and abetted Paul and Peter in preaching a gospel unconstrained by the Law. In Jerusalem and Palestine, each year saw things becoming much worse for the Christians. Antioch with the Syrian hinterland, however, Ephesus and Asia Minor as well as the Greek centres of civilization had not only long since been living under Rome's political shadow, but had been her cultural satellites also. Literally, "all roads led to Rome".

Peter knew himself to be the key-bearer of Christ's household, having special responsibility to look after its healthy growth to the limit of his power. This responsibility had been laid on him by the Lord himself, and most certainly he never discarded it. He could visit the more important churches, as once he did in Judaea and Samaria in order to act as mediator in the internal strife and to strengthen the disciples, and it can scarcely be a later invention that Peter spent some time on visitation in Antioch and in Corinth, out of which arose a "foundation",[290]

[289] Cf. Granderath: *op. cit.* 305 with 482.
[290] Antioch: Origen: *Hom. in Luc.* 6 c; Eusebius: *H. E.* III 36, 2; Chrysostom on Ignatius (the latter probably had a special knowledge of local tradition as a result of living many years in Antioch). Corinth: – Bishop Dionysius gives evidence of this about 170 (in Eusebius: *H. E.* II, 25, 8). Some scholars doubt the tradition concerning Antioch (see Cullmann: *Peter* p. 54) and concerning Corinth (pp. 55, 116), partly because they misinterpret the term "foundation", partly on account of the legendary

as otherwise reliable witnesses testify. As E. Caspar says, this is correct in the descriptive "higher sense" of the word "foundation". If we take as a basis the state of affairs suggested by the Biblical narrative: apostolic preaching and visitation,[291] then the foundation-legends receive their historical kernel, and the misunderstanding too, is explained, whereby later ages concluded from the *Cathedra Petri* and the missionary and organizational activity that Peter had been "bishop" of these churches: Caesarea, Antioch, Corinth, Rome. When he arrived in these places he found presbyter-bishops already active, and obviously he was their superior: apostolic authority embraced all that was meant in the first century by episcopal and presbyterial authority and in the second century by the authority of a bishop; but during the apostolic age, the word *episkopos* had not the same meaning as "bishop" had later. Or was Paul "monarchical bishop" of Derbe, Lystra, and Iconium, etc., because he installed *episkopoi* in these cities? Cullmann is correct when he proves that the title of "bishop" for Peter, especially when applied to Rome, appears only later on; [292] but he can rest assured that if, in later usage, the term has crept into literature – into apologetics for example, and says too little rather than too much of their

title "Peter, the first Bishop of . . ."; but more of this later. On the other hand, Tertullian: *Praescr.* 36, writes of the *cathedra*: "Go through the apostolic churches in turn, where the *cathedrae* of the apostles themselves still stand in their place." That is the chair of the liturgical celebrant on the east wall of the apse (Hermas: *M* 11), and in general the symbol of the teaching office (Ps.-Clement: *Epistle of Clement to James* 2; *Hom.* 3, 60 63; *Recogn.* 10, 71), and naturally Peter came from time to time as visitator to organize the congregations and provide them with suitable *episkopoi* (*Hom.* 29, 23; *Recogn.* 3, 63–74). Cf. C. Schmidt: *Studien . . .* 110; F. Probst: *Lehre u. Gebet in den ersten drei Jahrhunderten* (1871) 222 f. [291] Cf. Acts 9:32 ff. [292] *Peter* p. 234.

powers –, the term has not crept into the language of dogmatic pronouncements. It is quite possible that the legend of James the "bishop of Jerusalem" encouraged the use of the title "bishop of Rome" for Peter. Cullmann is wrong, however, when he asserts that this "late legend" about the Roman bishop, Peter, carries the least bit of weight against the succession of the Roman bishops in the Petrine supreme pastoral office.

To clarify this we must range a little wider. Let us consider: When Peter came to Rome the Christian congregation had already been there for a long time. There were already presbyter-bishops in Rome, and they did not lose their office on Peter's arrival, but now they were subject to Peter, as those had been in Antioch or Corinth when he paid his visits of whatever duration to those places.

Consider further that the title "bishop" *(episkopos)* in apostolic times was probably synonymous with "elder" *(presbyteros)*. This becomes obvious repeatedly in the New Testament. Acts 20:17 names as "bishops" the same people who later, in 20:28, are called "elders". Likewise the "bishops" of 1 Timothy 3:1 are equivalent to the "elders" of 1 Timothy 4:14; 5; 17; Titus 1:5; and the same thing can be found in Clement of Rome.[293] Every church had its presbyter-bishops; and there is evidence of this both in the Jewish-Christian church of Jerusa-

---

[293] Clement of Rome: *To the Corinthians* 42. On the early presbyter-bishops, see A. Michiel: *L'origine de l'Épiscopat* (1900); S. Dunin Borkowski in: Essèr-Mausbach: *Rel., Christent., Kirche* (²1914) 440 ff.; A. M. Koeniger in: *Festgabe f. A. Ehrhard* (1922) 285 (with literary references): B. Bartmann: *Lehrb. d. Dogma* II ⁸ 442; A. E. Feine: *Kirchl. Rechtsgesch.* I (1950); H. v. Campenhausen in: *Zts. f. Kirchengesch.* (1950–1) 133 ff., and *Kirchl. Amt* (1953) 23; J. Colson: *L'Évêque dans les communautés primitives* (1957); P. Gaechter in: *Zts. f. kath. Theol.* 1952 129 ff.

lem of Acts 11:30; 15:2; 21:18, and in the Pauline foundations of Acts 14:23; 20:17; and clearly there were no churches
without such presbyter-bishops. The contrary would have to be
rigourously proved.

In larger cities like Jerusalem and the Pauline city-congrega-
tions there were several presbyter-bishops, several "elders" or
"bishops" in the terminology of the time[294]. In smaller places
there might have been "one", and certainly each "house-
congregation" was looked after by one elder.[295] It is certain
that, in the period of the Pastoral Epistles, these presbyter-
bishops of a church in a city or district were supervised by someone authorized by the apostles. Titus and Timothy were superior
pastors set over a number of presbyter-bishops. Even from
the start, however, in each of the bigger city congregations, one
of these "elders" was probably responsible for unity amongst
his colleagues and within the congregation as a whole.[296]

[294] As well as the passages cited see Phil. 1:1; 1 Cor. 16:15–18; Acts
14:23; 20:17; 1 Thess. 5:12; Eph. 4:11; Heb. 13:17; 1 Tim. 4:14;
5:17; Tit. 1:5.
[295] See Rom. 16:3 along with my exposition in my edition of the
N.T.; also – 1 Cor. 16:19; Col. 4:15; Philem. 2.
[296] P. Gaechter (*Zts. f. kath. Theol.* 1952, 158–63) adduces good arguments which make it appear credible that the "monarchical" leadership
of the churches had "received its basis at least" in the apostolic age.
1. "Jesus in the midst of the Twelve and then in his commissioning of
Cephas as head of the Twelve" were the model of order within the
congregations; 2. Since Peter had appointed James leader of the Jerusalem church, Jerusalem had certainly had this one man at the head of
its presbytery; 3. When the monarchical episcopate emerges, there is
no trace of resistance or of any "struggle for power" within the presbytery. We might have expected this had there been any question of an
innovation. The research of L. Hertling in: *Biblica* 1939, 276 ff. is worthy
of note concerning the *primus inter pares* in the college of presbyters.

This office was usually reserved for the "first-fruit" of the congregation,[297] the one who as the first convert had opened the "door" to the Gospel by his example, and had brought others with him. L. Hertling[298] has proved of the supposedly "purely charismatic" congregation of Corinth, that it is highly probable that Stephanas, Fortunas, and Achaicus,[299] appointed by the apostle, preside, with Stephanas as their *primus inter pares*. Clement of Rome, who had the first Epistle to the Corinthians before him, and who had first-hand exact knowledge besides of the state of affairs in Corinth evidently regarded Stephanas as the head of the college of elders[300] whom the apostle had appointed, and who was succeeded after his death by Fortunas.[301] It is certain that in Jerusalem one man stood at the head of the whole presbytery: James, the Lord's kinsman. In our present study it can remain an open question whether he was a member of the Twelve from the beginning – identical with James the younger – or became a believer only after the Resurrection and then played a prominent part as president of the presbytery in the mother-congregation, and became a "pillar" of the young Church.[302]

---

[297] See 1 Cor. 16:15 along with the retrospective testimony of Clement of Rome (42). That the congregation had the right to nominate a candidate for ordination appears from the *Didache* 15 (election) and Clement 44 (consent of the congregation).

[298] *Biblica* 1939, 276ff.   [299] 1 Cor. 16:15ff.   [300] Clement 42.

[301] According to the conclusion of the *Epistle of Clement* (55), Fortunatus (of Corinth) along with the delegation is supposed to see to the settlement of the Corinthian dispute.

[302] Gal. 2:9. James is counted as one of the Twelve by Clement of Alexandria, Origen, Jerome and Catholic commentators in general. Many Protestant commentators like R. A. Lipsius, K. Holl, and O. Cullmann think this is only a retrospective association – and some Catholic exegetes too, like P. Gaechter (*op. cit.* 159), consider that this is "quite clear".

111

If this concept of the charismatic-hierarchical structure of the congregation is the correct one as early as the apostolic age – and the passages cited permit the conclusion – then, it is true, in the early period the "monarchical bishop", as one likes to call the principal pastor of a city congregation in the time of Ignatius of Antioch (c. 110), did not yet exist; and yet between the primitive stage and the later one there is no real cleavage, as some used to think – and still think. The adjective "monarchical" does not come from the documents, but has a secular, an almost objectionable sound about it. According to our sources, this "bishop", as he is now called to distinguish him from the "elders", is also surrounded by elders, and the ideal is that he along with these and the deacons should be an earthly copy of the Blessed Trinity in heaven[303], by virtue of their striving "to do all things in harmony with God". By contrast, there is only one difference of which there is an earlier trace, and that by no means shows any surrender or weakening of the brotherly, reciprocal relationship between bishop – presbyter – congregation. What appears is that leadership by a "bishop" emerges more distinctly – even "in the furthest lands";[304] and this is

[303] Ignatius: *Magn.* 6; *Ancient Christian Writers* 1946 Vol. 1, I, p. 70.
[304] Ignatius: *Eph.* 3. For this very reason we may not jump to the conclusion that in Philippi at that time there had been a presbytery without a presidential bishop, on the grounds that in Polycarp's letter to the Philippians (contemporary with Ignatius) there is a mention of presbyters but not of their bishop. This conclusion is drawn by A. v. Harnack: *Entstehung u. Entwicklung der Kirchenverfassung* (1910) 59, and by A. M. Koeniger in: *Festschrift f. A. Ehrhard* (1922) 285. This may very well contain a fresh indication that the "bishops" mentioned by Paul in Philippians 1:1 were also called "presbyters". In Paul's time they may have had a *primus inter pares,* superior to the rest only in jurisdiction. Cf. B. Bartmann: *Lehrb. d. Dogm.* II ⁸ 422.

caused clearly because of the growing danger of *gnosis,* and it manifests itself in a fresh definition of responsibilities, of which the nomenclature is in fact the sign.

The Pseudo-Clement may have given rise to the legend of James as bishop of Jerusalem, on the strength of this terminology; and others may have taken it over from him. The title is not appropriate in the apostolic age, for then "bishop" did not mean anything different from "elder". The leadership of the "elders" of Jerusalem may well have devolved upon James, and to that extent, following the later terminology, we might represent him as a "bishop" or even an "archbishop".[305]

As "founder" of the church in Antioch, according to the form of organization we have mentioned, Peter originally had no place in its list of bishops;[306] and the same might be said of his function as "bishop" of Rome. By Christ's commission he was supreme pastor of the whole church, wherever he happened to be. The title "bishop" of Rome might have been ascribed to him later, because it was known that he ended his days in Rome, and that his successor in the supreme pastorate at that time also happened to be the president of the presbytery and congregation of Rome – their "bishop", so men had come to say, in the sense of the "monarchical episcopate"; and because people had meanwhile forgotten that *episkopos* in the apostolic age did not mean the same as it did later. In the earliest lists of Roman bishops given by Irenaeus,[307] Peter and Paul appear as founders.

---

[305] *Recogn.* I, 43, 73.
[306] A. v. Harnack: *Chronol.* I, 199 ff., 208 ff.; E. Schwartz: *Kirchenge-schichte des Euseb.* III, CCXL ff.
[307] Irenaeus: *Adv. Haer.* III, 3, 3. Cf. Duchesne: *Liber Pontificalis* (1886) I (CCLX ff.); E. Caspar: *Die älteste röm. Bischofsliste (Festschr. f. P. Kehr,*

Irenaeus says nothing about Peter as "first bishop of Rome", but he does certainly trace the first bishop, Linus, back to Peter; and Linus is followed by Anacletus, Clement, and the rest.

c. Peter in Rome and his successors
as supreme pastors of the Church

Peter may have long remained undecided whether after his travels, to which Paul also alludes in 1 Corinthians 9:6, he would settle down permanently, and if so, where. It was a question of what was expedient for the work of the kingdom of God, not a question of theological necessity, rooted in the essence of the church or of the primacy. In the end of the day, however, there was only one city which could bear consideration as the centre of rising Christianity, the city which everyone of that age regarded as the centre of the world. When Cullmann says: "it is a fixed fact that *at that time,* in the sixth decade of the first century, Rome still played no leading rôle in the church at large, and Peter did not rule the entire church from Rome",[308] he has perhaps composed his sentence a little carelessly. What he should have written is: "It is not an established fact – that is, not directly attested – that at that time Peter led the church from Rome." All the same there are indications, as we have shown, and no positive evidence to cast doubt upon the reliability of the tradition. If the leaders had a more elaborate missionary plan than that reported in Galatians 2:9, then we might even surmise from Romans 15:20, "I did not want to build

1926); C. Schmidt: *Studien zu den Ps.-Klementinen* in: *TU* (1930) 335 ff.; E. Kohlmeyer in: *Th. Stud. u. Krit.* 1931, 230 ff.; B. Altaner: *Papstkataloge* in: *Lex. f. Theol. u. Kirche* VII, 939.
[308] *Peter* p. 234.

upon another man's foundation", that in the year 57–8 Paul knew that Peter was already in Rome or on his way there.[309] At all events, not much later, and following upon Peter's preaching,[310] St. Mark's Gospel and 1 Peter may both have been written in Rome at about the same date.

The death of the first apostle as Christ's witness and his baptism of blood jointly with Paul – whether simultaneously or not is uncertain[311] – raised Rome so high in the church's devotion that the question of succession in the Petrine office now came to concern the person but was no longer able to concern the see. We do not know if Peter himself explicitly appointed the person who was to succeed in his chair or if, after his death, the leading bishops of the church settled the matter by consultation amongst themselves or through ratification of an election by the Roman presbytery. The only thing of theological significance is that Peter had a successor as supreme pastor of the church.

Historically, the whole tradition of the early church is unambiguous and without a single contradiction concerning first, the martyrdom of Peter in Rome and second, his successors

---

[309] The latter in view of the circumstance that Romans 16 contains no hint of Peter's being in Rome. But to conclude from this (as H. Strathmann does in *Zts. f. system. Theol.* 1947, 246) that this possibility is "excluded", is unjustifiable, the more so because it is disputed whether Rom. 16 applies to Rome or to Ephesus. Romans 16:16, 25–7 might follow on from Romans 15:23, and the greeting might have been supplied from an epistle to the Ephesians now lost – in replacement of a missing passage.

[310] According to the evidence of Papias and of Clement of Alexandria in Eusebius: *H. E.* III, 39, 15; II, 15, 1.

[311] C. Schmidt: *Studien* . . . 361 ff.

in the Roman see. Obviously Rome might be destroyed or be lost to Christianity and the supreme pastor of the church would then be "bishop of Rome *in partibus infidelium*";[312] and obviously, the church might some day transfer the *Cathedra Petri,* in the person of its representative (Peter II), to some other region of the world. The "accident", humanly speaking – for it did not have to be so of necessity from the theological concept of the church –, the historical circumstance that the princes of the apostles eventually lived in Rome and died there, and also that Peter had somehow chosen this place, befell the Christian congregation in Rome and their bishops most opportunely, so that in fact no question at all was raised concerning the seat of the Petrine succession, and so that "the faithful everywhere"[313] turned to Rome to the "*Cathedra Petri,* the root and womb of Catholic unity"[314] – not only in practical, disciplinary, and charitable affairs,[315] but also because they knew that in the chair of Peter the normative rule of doctrinal tradition was guaranteed.[316] This was the chief reason for the numerous journeys to Rome which we know took place in the early centuries: the journeys of Justin, Irenaeus, Hegesippus, Tertullian, Origen, and of the leading advocates of disputed opinions likewise – Valentinus, Cerdo, Marcion, Apelles, Marcellina, Theodotus,

[312] Th. Granderath: *Gesch. d. Vatik. Konzils* III (1906) 28.
[313] Irenaeus: *Adv. Haer.* III, 3, 2.
[314] Cyprian: *Epistle* 48, 3.
[315] For example, the Corinthians to Clement in 96–7 and again by Bishop Dionysius to Soter about 170 (but cf. the letter in Eusebius: *H. E.* IV, 23, 9f.). Cf. A. v. Harnack: *The Expansion of Christianity* (1904) Book II, chap. 3, p. 187ff.
[316] Irenaeus: *Adv. Haer.* II, 3, 2.

Praxeas, Florinus, all in the second century, who went to seek the tolerance or favour of Rome.[317]

Ignatius of Antioch (c. 110) writes to the Roman church, using titles which exceed his customary measure of reverence. "To the church that has found mercy in the transcendent Majesty of the Most High Father and of Jesus Christ his only Son; . . . the church by the will of Him who willed all things that exist, beloved and illuminated through the faith and love of Jesus Christ our God; which also presides in the chief place of the Roman territory (the church of Rome was the apostolic church there, as, say, that of Antioch was in Syria), a church worthy of God, worthy of honour, worthy of felicitation, praise success, sanctification, and presiding in love maintaining the law of Christ, and bearer of the Father's name."[318] The meaning of the "pre-eminence (presidency) in love" has been much discussed. J. Thiele has shown that in the language of Ignatius "love" is very close to the biblical concept and signifies the moral-religious basis of the new life effected by the Spirit of Christ, the quintessence of the powers of grace which characterize the Christian life.[319] In this, Rome takes the "presidency" –

---

[317] See D. J. Unger in: *Theol. Studies* 1952, 410 f., who refers to detailed material by A. D. Doyle in: *Irish Eccl. Record* 1939, 298 ff.

[318] Text in *Ancient Christian Writers* (1946) Longmans Green Vol. 1, I, p. 80.

[319] J. Thiele in: *Th. u. Glaube* (1927) 705 ff. The once frequently used translation "President of the union of love" (the universal church) is scarcely accurate. See A. Ehrhard: *Die Kirche der Martyrer* (1932) 276; B. Altaner: *Patrology,* London, 1960 p. 108. Harnack's interpretation "President of love" = active charity (Berl. Sitz.-Ber. 1896, I, p. 120 ff.), as also the interpretation of J. Willig (in: *Hochland* II [1921] 257) – love-feast, is too narrow.

or has "pre-eminence" – and this is in keeping with the reference in the letter which follows, to her instructing other churches, and with the request that she take care of the Syrian church as Christ would and in the manner of a bishop.[320] Taking all this into account "there is no doubt that Ignatius places the Roman church at the head of all the churches",[321] as shortly before she had shown herself to be the superior of the church in Corinth – and Ignatius knew Clement's epistle.[322] Whence was this pre-eminence derived? The clue lies in one sentence: "I do not command you in the manner of Peter and Paul."[323] The fact that in this place he does not say in general, "like an apostle", as he does to the Trallians, but mentions the apostles' names, reveals that when thinking of Rome "the combined mention of Peter and Paul would 'necessarily' force itself upon a writer..."[324]

The epistle of the Roman bishop Clement to the Corinthians in the year 96 or 97 is highly significant concerning Rome's status as a capital city. It is remarkable how Cullmann softens this down: he reads out of the letter the exact opposite of what Emil Brunner did. For the latter, the distinctive thing in Clement is the concept of authority: the Corinthians are dealing with their bishop who appeals to "the legal right which has been secured through installation in the office".[325] Cullmann, on the other hand, finds merely the expression of sheer brother-

---

[320] In the same letter 3, 1 and 9, 1.
[321] A. Ehrhard: *Kirche der Martyrer* (1932) 276.
[322] O. Perler in: *Divus Thomas* 1944, 442f.
[323] 4, 1. [324] *Peter* p. 110.
[325] Emil Brunner: *The Misunderstanding of the Church* (1952) London, p. 78.

liness – the lack of which, according to Brunner reveals the vast gulf between Clement and Paul: "to exhort a divided sister church to harmony in a letter is not enough to establish one as the pope".[326] In fact Clement speaks in as brotherly a fashion as he possibly could, giving many reasons why the Corinthian trouble-makers should feel remorse. Cullmann is right on this point as against Brunner. Is Clement able to speak in any other way if he wishes to show himself the disciple of Peter, which he was? In the end, however, he cannot avoid adverting to his responsibilities, and this "authority" cannot be watered down. "But should any disobey what has been said by Him through us, let them understand that they will entangle themselves in transgression and no small danger. But for our part we shall be innocent of this sin."[327] Clement expounds the "accepted"[328] church order by saying that it was "sin" so to "renounce obedience at one's own discretion" to one appointed by the Spirit and in the same Spirit ordained after due testing, "so that he would have to resign". According to the church order of Hippolytus, even someone who has erred does not automatically lose his authority.[329] Only the court "which was able to give

---

[326] *Peter* p. 235.

[327] Clement of Rome: *Epistle to the Corinthians,* 59, text in Ancient Christian Writers (1946) Longmans Green, Vol. I, p. 45.

[328] H. v. Campenhausen: *Kirchl. Amt* 100f.

[329] Hippolytus: *Ref.* IX, 12, 21. Cf. A. M. Koeniger in: *Festschr. f. A. Ehrhard* (1922) 284. This rule, too, is in line with the Jewish conception of authority: Deut. 17:11 demands respect for the priest. "All are to obey the priest's decision", we read in the statues of the congregation of Damascus. "Early Christianity at first recognized this theory of the ministry (Matt. 23:2f.; John 11:51) and then took it over (Luke 22:32; John 21:15; Gal. 2:6)" says E. Stauffer, who quotes texts from Luther in the same vein. See *Zts. f. Religions- und Geistesgeschichte* 1952, 201.

him authority in God's name is able to deprive him of it in the same name".[330] The congregation is not thereby "disfranchised as it were" with regard to their pastors "or subjected to an authoritarian ecclesiastical regime: no matter how determined Clement may be to protect the rights of office-bearers, the presumption is always taken for granted that these, for their part, should never allow themselves to become guilty of anything, but blamelessly fulfil their duty".[331] Moreover the people of the general priesthood, that is those who have the gifts of the spirit in the "church built upon the foundation of the apostles and the prophets",[332] obviously possess a share in the formation of judgment; and later history teaches us that when these are subjected to "oppression, on principle (more correctly from time to time in actual fact), far-reaching results are bound to ensue".[333]

How does it come about that "Rome" – it is the congregation through its bishop which writes to the congregation at Corinth– calls to order the trouble-makers in another congregation, appoints a special delegation to restore order, in the name of Christ? Clearly because someone there like Peter knew himself to be responsible for the unity of the church. And Clement acted exactly as Peter in 1 Peter 5:2–3 had required that a pastor should act: with authority and with love, "not as lording it over the clergy, but, being made a pattern of the flock, from the heart". The Corinthians accepted the admonition from Rome in this spirit, and in the time of their bishop Dionysius in 170 were still reading Clement's epistle as through it were a

[330] K. Müller: *Kirchengesch.* I, 1 (³1941), 271.
[331] H. v. Campenhausen: *Kirchl. Amt.* 101.
[332] Eph. 2:20.   [333] H. v. Campenhausen: *Kirchl. Amt* 328.

portion of holy Scripture.[334] "No other church has presented itself with such lustre upon the scene of church history as the Roman church, through the so-called Epistle of Clement."[335]

Clement stood in a line of development stretching from the Pastoral Epistles, through Ignatius to Origen in the East and Cyprian in the West, and which is assessed in essentially the same way by different scholars. F. C. Grant: *An Introduction* (1950) and H. v. Campenhausen: *Kirchliches Amt* (1953) may be taken as typical. The development of the church, precipitated by dispute with the Gnostics, is characterized on the one hand by the initial collection of the New Testament Scriptures, on the other by an increasing concentration of official energies, but both in order to preserve and protect the revealed mystery. If we follow v. Campenhausen in thinking that the road to the Catholicism of the second and third centuries ran astray into a certain "one-sided officialdom" to which "the ecclesiastical mind inclines at all times in any case",[336] we should observe also that v. Campenhausen like F. C. Grant is in no doubt that the rigid church life of the second and third centuries has "its beginnings" in the first,[337] and that the required defence against the Gnostic threat could scarcely have assumed a different form.

Ecclesiastical office is that very "judiciary which comes into the front of the picture in this activity".[338] "Amidst all the confusion of fanatical movements, accretions and schisms during

---

[334] *Epistle of Dionysius* in Eusebius: *H. E.* 23, 11.
[335] A. v. Harnack: *Dogmengeschichte* ⁴486.
[336] H. v. Campenhausen: *op. cit.* 325.
[337] F. C. Grant: *An Introduction* 294.
[338] H. v. Campenhausen: *op. cit.* 87; cf. 198.

the Gnostic crisis the church was acutely conscious of the danger of having her links with the past severed. As a result she laid prime stress upon the preservation of her original teaching and tradition .... Authority is not asserted for its own sake, but primarily because it is supposed to be of service in the necessary conservation of the primitive tradition and in the protection of a legitimate continuity of the gospel."[339] We may regret that in the process the free operation of the Spirit, which the *Didache,* Justin, and Hermas recall with a certain pride,[340] was correspondingly forced into the background. This was certainly "not the result of a special priestly will to rule"; on the contrary,[341] the whole development can be seen in the light

[339] H. v. Campenhausen: *op. cit.* 328.

[340] *Didache* 11 and 13; Justin: *Dial.* 82, 1; Hermas: *M.* 11, 5 ff.

[341] H. v. Campenhausen: *op. cit.* On the other hand it is doubtful whether in this context v. Campenhausen thinks that he detects "a more deep-seated change in the faith itself" behind the whole movement in the second and third centuries. "The primitive meaning of evangelical authority begins to become obscured. Now the church is no longer living, in a radical sense, from the forgiveness of Christ, and it understands its holiness as a human task which is demanded of Christians and which they must fulfil." It is a questionable presupposition that the meaning of the church is simply identical with the message of forgiveness. As Berdyaev suggested in *The Meaning of the Creative Act,* that might very well lead to an anthropocentric doctrine of happiness as the quintessence of Christianity. And, with regard to the "works" of penance for grave sin which the ecclesiastical power of the keys prescribed in those times (to which Campenhausen seems to allude), an opinion or custom of pastoral theology – to some extent the creation of its own age – within the limited sphere of the church's penitential practice, need not by any means touch the nerve of faith in redemption, and besides, it may remind us, even if in a lop-sided fashion, of our Lord's own praise of works of penance (Luke 10:13) and of God's intention of sanctifying those whom he has justified (Rom. 6:19; 2 Cor. 6:6; etc.).

of a divine providence by anyone who is able to see events not from the purely historical level, but with the eye of faith. F. C. Grant writes: "If one believes, as I certainly do, that the development of the ministry was in accordance with the mind and will of God, it must be viewed as the result of divine overruling and of the guidance of the Holy Spirit – rather than as the setting up of a predetermined organization."[342]

Irenaeus of Lyons wrote his great work about a hundred years after Clement. From his youth a member of the circle of St. John the apostle, and in lively touch with the churches in East and West, he defended the tradition he had received against those who contested the Christian faith. The material which is relevant to our present purpose is contained in the first three chapters of the third book.

Whoever wishes to see Christian truth as against its aberrations, can find it in the tradition derived from the apostles in every bishop's church. Their lists of bishops bear witness every time to the continuity of apostolic tradition. "We can enumerate those who were appointed bishops in the churches by the apostles, and their successors (or successions) down to our own day, who never taught, and never knew, absurdities such as these men produce." (That is, like the alleged esoteric doctrines of the leaders of the Gnostic sects.)

Instead of making a detailed interrogation of all the episcopal church, however, in order to be convinced of the unity of Christian tradition of faith, it is simpler to do this by "pointing to the apostolic tradition and the faith that is preached to men, which has come down to us through the succession of bishops;

[342] F. C. Grant 294.

the tradition and creed of the greatest, the most ancient church, the church known to all men, which was founded and set up at Rome by the two most glorious apostles, Peter and Paul. For with this church, because of its position of leadership and authority, must needs agree every church, that is, the faithful everywhere; for in her the apostolic tradition has always been preserved by the faithful from all parts." "The rest, who stand aloof from the primitive succession and assemble in any place whatever, we must regard with suspicion, . . ."[343]

The Roman bishops after Peter and Paul are these: Linus, Anacletus, Clement, Evaristus . . .

In chapter 2 the term "foundation" is explained by the following "instituted". It was the common practice of congregations which once had an apostle in their midst to refer to themselves as apostolic foundations. Chapter 3 contains the oldest Roman list of bishops, for Hegesippus only indicates their existence without quoting the individual names.[344] The context shows us what attracts Irenaeus' interest: the list of succession is important to him because they guarantee the coherence, the spiritual

[343] Text of Irenaeus in *Documents of the Christian Church,* World's Classics, pp. 96, 97, 99. For an exposition of the much-discussed second section, see Batiffol-Seppelt: *Urkirche u. Katholizismus* (1910); A. Ehrhard: *Die Kirche der Martyrer* (1932); and, with particular thoroughness, D. J. Unger in: *Th. Studies* 1952, 359–418. On the third section containing the oldest catalogue of Roman bishops see above n. 401.

[344] His account of his own visit of investigation to Rome (in Eusebius: *H.E.* IV, 22, 3) is earlier than the evidence of Irenaeus, but in fact tells us less. Celsus, too, *later* than Irenaeus, knew the Roman list (Origen: *Contra Cels.* V. 62). On the later list of Epiphanius (*Pan. h.* 27, 6), see C. Schmidt: *Studien* . . . 336 ff. On Rufinus's list in his introduction to the translation of Ps.-Clement, see C. Schmidt: *op. cit.* 350. Eusebius the historian is right when he relies upon Irenaeus (*H.E.* III, 4, 9; 15, 21; V, 6, 1).

124

unity of the doctrine which is handed on. He wrote the above text about the year 180, but had visited Rome a few years earlier. "The line of argument he follows against those who deny the authority of the Bible, is clear and effective."[345]

[345] H. v. Campenhausen: *Kirchl. Amt* 186. That the bishops were even more important than Scripture as an assurance of traditional doctrine, is stressed also by: D. van den Eynde: *Les normes de l'enseignement chrét. dans la lit. patr. des trois premiers siècles* (1939) 161; H. Holstein: *La tradition des Apôtres chez S. Irénée,* in *Rev. Sc. rel.* 1949, 229 ff. That Hegesippus was the first to give the notion of apostolic succession (including the Petrine) a special "technical meaning", church apologetics having introduced the formal notion of the *diadoche* (transmission of office from hand to hand) – with lists of bishops to prove an unbroken chain of authority back to the apostles – from the Gnostics in order to outdo the Gnostic succession (H. v. Campenhausen: *op. cit.* 172 ff.) is a view requiring not only historical correction (see n. 256) but theological distinctions as well. It is true that in these days apologetics had been quick to use the lists of bishops to prove that the apostolic tradition rested in more reliable hands than did the esoteric teaching of the Gnostics; but the apostolic succession is older than Hegesippus and in essence is not bound up with the demonstration of an unbroken list of bishops. Authority in the church always rests upon the ordination by the Holy Spirit through lawful office-bearers, and presuming a corresponding disposition of faith in the recipient. It would seem that v. Campenhausen exaggerates the rôle of those who ordain in the Catholic view of succession. Their rôle is, in fact, the same as that of those who baptize. Baptism is the fundamental ordination to the priesthood of all believers. Neither baptism nor ordination creates a human causal connection resembling a kind of spiritual heredity passing from those who ordain to the ordinands. The true ordainer is the Holy Spirit, the *minister sacramenti* for the time being is only a human instrument. Moreover, v. Campenhausen seems to make the objective essential form of apostolic succession (transmission of authority from the apostles to those enrusted by them, and so on from these to others) dependent upon the historical demonstration of spiritual succession in the particular sees. But even if, for example, the Roman list of bishops of Hegesippus is "no more reliable than the hundred-year memory of the Roman congregation", the author-

Ancient Christian evidence tells us primarily of the actual precedence of Rome, not of any theological reasons for it. We must be on our guard, therefore, of projecting back to the early period, concepts which are today associated with the papacy – the tiara, the sedan, and the rest. The mode of function, as B. Bartmann says, "the exercise of the primacy" ought not to be judged by modern standards,[346] for it might be that the same principle of *syntaxis,* the organization in a unity,[347] in those days, was more of a *confaederatio christiana* under Peter, whereas later a more rigid centralization emerged.

We can seek in vain amongst the apostolic fathers and the first apologists for biblical-theological reasons for the hierarchical Petrine order. This might be disconcerting, and not a few critics, from the polemics of H. Koch to the irenic O. Cullmann take this as a proof that the succession to Peter in the office of supreme pastor of the whole church did not come at all within the scope of early Christian thought.[348] But that is to deceive oneself. Can we expect to find a "biblical theology" before there was a canon of Scripture? As Harnack proves, [349] Justin

ity of the Roman bishop did not originate with the retrospective labours of Hegesippus, and does not depend upon the accuracy of his list of names. Or what bishop would find it necessary to trace his spiritual ancestry back to the apostles? Nor can it be concluded from the circumstance that the original presbyter-bishops were not yet monarchical bishops, that it was impossible to place the later bishops in the same series as the first presbyter-bishops. The jurisdiction of the presbyter-bishop may not have been so comprehensive as that of the later bishop, the hierarchical grade is the same in both periods and does not move from a lower to a higher.

[346] B. Bartmann: *Dogmatik* II[8] 169.
[347] Council of Chalcedon in Denzinger: *Ench.* n. 149.
[348] *Peter* p. 239.
[349] Harnack: *Die Entstehung des N.T.* (1914) 12 151.

clearly did not know of one. He would have fared much better in his argument with Trypho had he been able to appeal to an accepted document of the Christian faith. The collection of the four gospels first began to be made in Asia Minor about the middle of the second century. Then, as protection against the Gnostics, the chief churches from the west coast of Asia Minor to Rome, working together and keeping in the fullest contact, made sure of a more extensive collection which included the most important of the apostolic epistles. At the end of the second century a canon of "the books of the new Covenant" had been accepted in Rome according to the Catholic-apostolic norm, a norm which "because of its intrinsic worth and the authority of the Roman church" was gradually accepted by the other churches as well.[350] Hitherto the apostolic doctrinal tradition had been collected in the "Apostles' Creed" and guaranteed by the authority of the successors of the apostles, a shield of Christian truth against unrestrained gnosis and the "confused complex" of secret revelations, pseudo-Gospels, legends of the apostles and so on. Not until the beginning of the third century was theology in a position to allow the New Testament, clearly circumscribed, to serve as evidence of divine revelation. From that time onwards the Church's apostolic doctrinal tradition and the New Testament form, as it were, "the foci of an ellipse", a spiritual realm against the power of which the arrows of Gnosticism rebound.

Irenaeus may serve as an illustration of what has been said. He stands in the last phase of the development we have just sketched, in which the living teaching authority based upon

[350] Harnack: *op. cit.* 76.

the apostolic succession on the one hand, and the Scriptures on the other, begin to act as a counter-balance to each other. What do we find in Irenaeus? When he speaks so as to affect the heart and mind of the people with edifying instruction, as in the so-called "Proof of apostolic preaching",[351] one receives a deep impression of the biblical inspiration of the great bishop's piety. "So he has increased, through our faith in him, our love towards God and our neighbour, rendering us godly and just and good . . . ." The redeemed are "to go free in newness by the Word, through faith and love towards the Son of God", for the Son of God "was seen on earth and conversed with men, joining and uniting the Spirit of God the Father with what God had fashioned, so that man became according to the image and likeness of God."[352] He makes copious use of the Scriptures of the Old and the New Testament, although all that matters to the faithful in practice, as it is put at the end of the "preaching of the truth", is that they hold fast to the way of life. "This is the way of life . . . handed over by the apostles and handed down by the church in the whole world to her children. This must be kept in all security, with good will, and by being well pleasing to God through good and sound moral character."[353] But when Irenaeus is speaking as theologian in his *Against Heresies,* and undertakes to prove the Christian truth against those who dispute it, how does he attack the gnosis, what does he take as the rule and instrument of Christian truth? Is it Scripture? He could scarcely do much with that, for those who follow Marcion accept only a fraction of

[351] Text in *Ancient Christian Writers* (1952) Longmans Green Vol. XVI.
[352] Ibid. chap. 87, 89, 97. [353] Ibid. chap. 98.

the Bible, and the rest, those in Egypt and east Jordania, for example, use their own adaptations of the revealed Scriptures. Again others, the "enlightened", interpret Scripture in their own way, appealing to "hidden mysteries which they taught the perfect in private and in secret".[354] Against these the church turned for support to "those who were appointed bishops in the churches by the apostles and their successors (or successions) down to our own day, who never taught, and never knew, absurdities such as these men produce".

If the apostles had known of any esoteric doctrines (for the 'perfect'), then they would have handed these on to those men to whom they entrusted the churches, rather than to any others. In a later passage we read: "Therefore we ought to obey only those presbyters who are in the church, who have their succession from the apostles, as we have shown; who with their succession in the episcopate have received the sure gift of the truth according to the pleasure of the Father. The rest, who stand aloof from the primitive succession, and assemble in any place whatever, we must regard with suspicion either as heretics and evil-minded; or as schismatics, puffed up and complacent; or again as hypocrites, acting for the sake of gain and vainglory. All these have fallen from the church."[355] Thus the basic theological norm is this: "The teaching of the apostles is the true gnosis. And we have the ancient constitution of the church universal, and the character of the Body of Christ in the succession of the bishops . . . with its safeguard of the Scriptures in the fullness and soundness of their interpretation, without addition

[354] Irenaeus: *Adv. Haer.* III, 1. *Documents of the Christian Church* p. 96.
[355] Ibid. IV, 26, 2. Text in *Documents of the Christian Church* p. 98 f.

of subtraction an untampered text with a lawful and careful scriptural exposition, and the supreme gift of love, which is more excellent than all other gifts."[356]

As we see, apostolic teaching authority, Scriptures, and love stand in a reciprocal relation; and Irenaeus is hardly capable of giving a rational exposition of the various factors and of comparing them one with the other. The practical rule is simple as the following makes clear: "Seeing that we have so many proofs, there is no need to seek among others for the truth which we can so easily obtain from the church . . . . And if the apostles had not even left us the Scriptures, would it not behove us to follow the order of tradition which they handed on to those to whom they entrusted the churches?"[357]

[356] Ibid. IV, 33. Text in *Early Church Classics* (1916) S. P. C. K., *The Treaties of Irenaeus Against the Heresies,* Vol. II, p. 67 f., trs. Hitchcock.

[357] Ibid. III, 4. Text in same source, p. 87 f. Tertullian is interesting who, some thirty years later than Irenaeus, in the central portion of his "preface to case against heretics" (*praescr.* 14–37) argues in exactly the same way as Irenaeus, whom he obviously has before him. "(14): The faith has been set down in the rule of faith (the Apostles' Creed). If now the heretics argue from Scripture, how else could they speak of the faith? – (15): thus we come here to our particular topic. We have to find out who is competent to claim holy Scripture as their own. (16–18): The heretics treat the Scriptures according to their own inclination: result – Scripture against Scripture. (19): Hence one cannot appeal to Scripture without first asking: to whom does Scripture belong, by whom, when, and to whom was the doctrine given, through which we are made Christians? (28): The Catholic churches are off-shoots of the apostolic Church. They are all *one,* that is the original one of the apostles, from which they all stem. Hence they have communion with each other. There is no other ultimate foundation for these rules of behaviour than the single tradition of the same faith. (32): The sectaries may produce the genealogies of their own churches, they may show the lists of their bishops which, following

These texts may have made it plain that we cannot expect to find twentieth-century biblical theology in the early centuries. Scripture, the components of which were guaranteed by tradition, was primarily an instrument of edification, and only through the passage of time became *instrumentum doctrinae*. Meditation upon the faith contented itself with the authority of the teaching office which guaranteed Christian truth; and yet the succession of bishops, especially those of Rome, going back to the apostles, to Peter, brought men close to the Lord, to the Word of God himself. In fact the Scriptures themselves only came into existence in this way, as far as their human aspect is concerned. To try to prove any Christian truth at all solely from Scripture, independently of the authority of the mother who had brought forth the Scriptures from her womb – so to speak – would have seemed to any of the ancient theologians to be striking at air. No Church – no Bible. The Bible is the child of mother church by the Holy Spirit. If that is the way things are, then it need not seem strange that there was no hurry to produce a Scriptural proof for the primacy of the Roman bishop. And when, at the beginning of the third century, people began to quote the text of Matthew about Peter the rock, this was not done for apologetic reasons at all, as if to justify the ecclesiastical office to outsiders, but, as shall shortly

the principle of succession, reach from the beginning down to the present. (36): Very well then, go through the apostolic churches in turn, where the *cathedrae* of the apostles themselves stand, where one can read the genuine lists. (37): The heretics, then, cannot be allowed to appeal to Scripture: we can prove without Scripture that they have no part in the Scriptures. Because they have not a succession joined with the apostles, their doctrines are not of Christ, and they have no legal claim to the Christian Scriptures."

become clear, for spiritual reasons – the deepening of church unity.

For the rest, is it really so striking that theoretical proofs of the primacy were so long wanting? In the *Didascalia,* the Syrian church *ordo* of the third century, the "monarchical bishop" appears in all his authority and is highly praised for his dignity; but we seek in vain in this comprehensive work for any biblical-theological justification, or for any kind of justification whatsoever, of this office. Because of the absence of theological proof, then, may we conclude that the monarchical episcopate "had not at that time existed at all in religious consciousness"? Another point: the church before Constantine's time, facing the constant threat of persecution, had "other things to worry about than controversy over the primacy".[358]

The first text to which appeal was made in support of the Petrine power to bind and loose was the classic Matthew 16:17ff.; and it was probably Pope Callixtus (217–222)[359] who applied it.

---

[358] C. Schmidt: *Studien* 330.

[359] *Peter* p. 166. "Probably" – we might equally well say "perhaps"; for it is doubtful whether the "bishop of bishops" of Tertullian is in fact Callixtus. It would seem that Tertullian is aiming his ironical polemic against his own Bishop Agrippinus (see G. Esser: *Der Adressat der Schrift Tertullians De pud.* (1914); K. Adam: *Das sog. Bussedikt des Papstes Kallistus* (1917); B. Altaner: *Die Ecclesia Petri propinqua,* in: *Th. Rev.* (1939) 129ff.; B. Poschmann: *Poenitentia* I (1940) 348ff.; B. Poschmann: *Busse u. letzte Ölung* (*Handb. der Dogmengesch.* IV, 3 [1951] 21f.). The Church was concerned with resisting the Montanist severity in public penance. That the saying about the keys in Matt. 16 (and about "binding" and "loosing" in Matt. 16 and 18) gave to the authorities in the church not only responsibility for teaching and for worship but also power to order public penance (power to forgive in Christ's name), is founded in the Bible and had already been mentioned (see above), but the provocation of Montanism

Soon after, ironically, it was used by Pseudo-Clement to make it clear that he wrote as a Catholic in spite of the Judaistic flavour of his novel. "To the Lord James, president of the holy church of the Hebrews" he makes Clement of Rome, his hero, write as follows:

"Be it known to you, my Lord, that Simon, who was appointed foundation of the church on account of his true faith and the firm basis of his doctrine, and so received the new name of Peter from the infallible lips of Jesus himself: he was the first-fruit of our Lord, first among the apostles..., and he came as far as Rome and, saving men by his teaching, which was pleasing to God, exchanged his earthly life for a violent death. In the days just before his death he assembled the brethren and addressed the whole congregation: 'The day of my death is approaching, as I have learned from him who sent me, the Lord and Master, Jesus Christ, therefore I appoint this Clement to be your bishop. To him I

now forced it into a phase of theoretical justification (see J. Ludwig: *Die Primatworte Matt. 16:18, 19 in der altkirchl. Exegese* [1952]). That the episcopal (priestly) power to forgive corresponded to the "urgent desire for salvation" of the faithful, is certainly true, but only receives a theological basis if, in cases of *grave* sin, "the evangelical meaning of all Christian authority" is embodied in the "official order" (cf. v. Campenhausen: *op. cit.* 260). The probability that Callixtus used Matthew 16 – as Cullmann asserts – seems heightened by the circumstance that Ps.-Clement very likely alludes to Callixtus as his literary precursor: – C. Schmidt: *Studien* 106. It is certain, however, that Matt. 16 plays a part in the discussion between Cyprian and Stephen I some thirty years later (254–7) on the validity of "heretical baptism". Cyprian was not pleased with the appeal to the text of Matthew in support of the succession in the chair of the Pope alone (*Epistle* 75, 16f.), but he had no wish to oppose this interpretation directly (see E. Caspar: *Primatus Petri* in: *Zts. d. Savigny Stiftg.* 1927, 315).

entrust my *cathedra* of preaching and hand on to him the power to bind and to loose, so that what he ordains on earth shall be decreed in heaven also .... But you (Clement) I charge to send to James, the brother of our Lord, all my sermons. It will be a consolation to him to know that the man who is taking over the chair of doctrine after me is one who has been well-instructed and is acquainted with saving discourse.'"

It is certainly not a burning concern of the author of the *Pseudo-Clementina* to make propaganda for the papacy in his native land – presumably in the East; but that he knew of the Petrine power to bind and to loose as the "canon of the church", that is as its basic rule, is stated quite plainly.[360] The fictional dress of the book does not cancel the significance of this evidence, nor does the error that Peter was immediately succeeded by Clement – which may have been a device of the novelist's licence to enhance the importance of his hero in the reader's eyes.[361] In the *Pseudo-Clementina* the evidence of the Petrine office is closely bound up with evidence concerning the episcopal office. In the introductory *Letter of Clement to James* it is taken for granted; but it is again specially sub-

---

[360] *Epistle of Clement to James*, 2. H. Waitz: *Die Ps.-Klementinen* (1904) 65, and C. Schmidt: *Studien* ... 123, have also pointed this out.

[361] The novelist was interested not in history but in the religious edification and entertainment of his reader; but his contemporaries and successors took him seriously, and hence Epiphanius and Rufinus likewise had great difficulty in harmonizing the obvious contradiction concerning Clement's "immediate" succession with the Roman list of bishops in Irenaeus (see C. Schmidt: *Studien* ... 336 ff. 350 ff.). It remains credible nonetheless that Clement was ordained by Peter himself, as a presbyter that is, years before the death of the apostle (see Tertullian: *Praescr.* 4, 32). This will also be the historical nucleus of the combination which Rufinus attempted in order to bring Linus as well as Cletus (Anacletus) and Cle-

stantiated in the homilies. God who rules all things has arranged all things in order: He desires also to educate men through order in both the natural and the spiritual spheres. Hence he has appointed some to lead and some to be led, but not in such a manner that[362] the community exists for the sake of its "lords", but so that the leaders conceive of their commission as a "service" – nothing more. Into Peter's mouth is put the moral exhortation which accompanies the installation of Bishop Zachaeus of Caesarea: "I know full well", Peter adresses him, "what labours I expect you to have because of this, and I know that you shall become the object of the critical judgment of many whom none can ever succeed in pleasing. But if you do what is right you will earn all the more the good pleasure of God. Therefore I beseech you, accept the task with great courage for the sake of God, for the sake of Christ, and for the salvation of the brethren."[363]

This address of "Peter" occurs in the more substantial sections of this curious book which has occupied our attention for some time. Its concluding thoughts suggest the theme which we also might take as our conclusion. In the Byzantine liturgy there is a prayer for Monday of Holy Week which is worthy of note. This prayer asks for the Spirit of Christ for the holy ministry[364]:

"Too small-minded, O Lord, to discern the ineffable my-

---

ment in touch with Peter. He asserts indeed: "accepimus" (we were able to learn): Preface to *Recogn.* (cf. C. Schmidt: *Studien* . . . 350). But that Linus and Cletus (Anacletus) led the Roman church *in the life-time* of the apostle, and Clement after his death, was a theory which Rufinus most likely thought out with an eye on Ps.-Clement.

[362] *Hom.* 3, 61f.

[363] *Hom.* 3, 64.

[364] *Triodion Katanyktion* (Rome 1879) 623. Cf. K. Kirchhoff: *Die Ostkirche betet*, IV, 62f.

stery of your plan of redemption, the mother of the sons of Zebedee besought you to grant her sons the honours of a worldly kingdom.

But instead of that, you promised your friends that they should drink the cup of death;

and yourself desired to drink, before they did, the cup which purifies from sin.

We cry to you, O Saviour of our souls. To you be praise!

You desire to know, O Lord, that your disciples have a pure mind: 'Act not as the heathen do, desiring to lord it over the weak.

Let it not be so amongst you, my disciples, for from love I have become small.

Let the first amongst you be the servant of all, let the lord be as the subject,

and let him who holds a place of honour be as the last. For I myself have come to serve poor Adam, to give my life as the ransom-price for all who call upon me.' – To you be the praise!''

If we will only reflect a little on the history of the church, we cannot avoid the impression that, for great stretches of history and on a large scale, there have always been some who thought much of themselves and took up the strain of the request of the sons of Zebedee – although these self-conceits are of no significance, for God is no respecter of persons.[365] There is no call upon any of us to judge others, but we need not cover up what is clearly visible.

[365] Gal. 2:6.

In the essay in which W. Soloviev gave his reasons for attaching himself to the chair of Peter without at the same time leaving the Orthodox church of his birth,[366] he speaks of a "papal imperialism" which – in spite of its cultural benefits for Western civilization – in the religious sense was a disaster, a deformation of Christ's intention concerning the hierarchical element in the church. Hadrian VI frankly admitted of the rift in the Church that not a few "reprobates" ruled in the Roman Curia, and that "perhaps this whole evil (the Reformation the rift then threatening for the first time) derives from this."[367] In spite of all their respect for the religious qualities which have inhered in the Petrine Chair during the past generations, non-Catholic Christians believe that they can still see, in the modern shape of Roman centralization, traces of a system of "power politics". Admittedly this is immeasurably more refined than in earlier days, but is still nonetheless real. And so in Christ's name they find it "impossible" to be convinced that Peter, the disciple of Jesus, can be set alongside Peter II, the Roman papacy. This is the tragic reality which one must face from the Catholic side in order not to cherish false hopes.

However things may appear in God's eyes, in those of men the concept of the Petrine office is burdened by the *history* of that office. In other words, the whole difficulty of the problem is not primarily theological but derives from history, and works itself out in a psychological fear which one would have to face if one committed oneself to Peter II. It is of little help to justify author-

---

[366] W. Soloviev: *La Russie et l'Église universelle* (1899) p. LVI.
[367] *Analecta hist. Hadriani VI* (1727) 375 ff.; L. v. Pastor: *Hadrian VI* (1907) 93 f.

ity in the church from the Bible and the early church, no matter how necessary that may be: the theology of the primacy appears as an ideology and is ineffective as long as the ghost of the "other", who once tempted Jesus, stands on the fringe of imagination, with the according threat to Christian freedom.

To a well-disposed person I once pointed out a saying of Leo the Great that the dignity of the office is said to shine out all the more, *"ubi sic summorum servatur autoritas, ut in nullo inferiorum putetur imminuta libertas* (where the authority of the superior is so maintained that the freedom of none of his subjects seems to be diminished)."[368] He smiled and I knew what he wanted to say. It would be naïve to think that sentiments or convictions of the heart can be removed by theological arguments. The wise author of the first sentences in the *Irenikon*[369] says of Soloviev: "He was convinced that, in human estimation, a purely historical or juridical argument in support of the Petrine primacy would be bound to remain ineffective"; and for this reason he had appealed to the "heart" of his Slav compatriots. "The holy ministry is love; it has its foundation in love alone; its sole function is love." This may indeed be true, but who cannot see that it lies in the realm of the ideal: suspicion and scepticism, however, turn to the embodiment of the idea.

If striving for unity is a command of Christ and cannot be separated from Christian life, then Catholics may not rest content with proving the validity of the hierarchy and expecting others to examine their consciences. Catholics will have to make their own contribution. There is need for a "conversion" on both

---

[368] Leo I: *Ep*. 120: Migne *PL* 54, 1048.
[369] *Irénikon* 1926, 74.

sides. Certainly, "conversion" (self-examination, penance, readiness to change) will, in this case always have a particular significance for the different participants, but for essentially the same objective reasons. If some might have to reconsider, for Christ's sake, the question of the completeness of their faith, others, for Christ's, might make a beginning with perfect justice, brotherly love, freedom within what God permits. For all, however, in the same folly of the Cross, which the worldly-wise onlooker doubtless ridicules as "romanticism", penance means what it has always meant: surrender of pride, the sacrifice of humanly selfish or collectively selfish insistence on particular human traditions. In the Catholic sphere it is probably above all insistence on habits of human church laws which causes non-Catholics to think in terms of a Roman Catholic "system" in breach with the Spirit of Christ, the Spirit of service and of love. In that respect we are certainly also to blame if unity of the Church is not achieved. Much of what has jeopardized it, at least hitherto, cannot be supported by an appeal to a "divine law".

Let us suppose that one day "Peter, Paul, and John" – the symbolic figures in Soloviev's legend of Antichrist – recognize of one another that those who are in good faith desire but to follow Christ alone and to honour his revelation as the sole rule of what is Christian, and that to demand any other rule for the community of brethren would be to cast doubts upon one's own position. Let us further suppose that the separate individuals ("Peter, Paul, and John") honestly discover that through this common faith and by virtue of the seal of baptism they all belong to the One Church, but were unfortunately estranged from each other by mutual divisions. Suppose also that, they would truthfully realize and admit that the division was not, or is not, caused by the defection of one guilty party from another innocent party, but signifies a common guilt in different rôles. Through these realizations they would discover and admit that they did not have to reproach one another, but only to respect and love each other mutually, for the sake of Christ; they would thus return to the unity of the Church, as a result of each turning to the common Lord. Being with him, they are also close to each other. In reality, this means a great deal for all of us. Above all, that there can be no quarrel over status amongst the disciples. That would occur only if for a time the disciples were not "with the Lord". But in his presence none of this can happen. And if one imagines himself to be important and has indeed a special calling in Christ's name, then he would make himself small before the rest. Peter washes John's and Paul's feet, because the Lord washed his. Arguments over precedence, claims to personal glory and similar points only matter "when love grows cold".[370] Jesus counted on this – but not as one of the fruits of his Spirit. Hence the resolution of the problem of the primacy is not – today and for the future at least – primarily a theological question nor a juridical question. It is above all a question of the heart: "Peter, do you love me, –more than these?" For Peter (including Peter II and so on) the question of the primacy is primarily a question about the seriousness of the imitation of him who "was equal to God but emptied himself, taking the form of a servant"[371]; and this quite apart from the responsibility laid upon him by Christ for the whole church. For the others it is a question about the same humility and love of the Lord and, for his sake, of unity with the "presidency of love" – to use Ignatius'

---

[370] Matt. 24:12.   [371] Phil. 2:6–7.

description of the Romans. When the heart, brotherly love, prepares the way, knowledge can follow, but not otherwise. *Amando cognoscimus.*

And so, in our Christian hope that springs from faith, "Peter, Paul, and John" – the leaders of the separated communities – will one day meet and speak concerning Christian unity. It will be done for Christ's sake. It is not only those "below", but those "at the top" who must prepare the way, so that the people in the separated communities do not lag spiritually behind when the leaders are meeting. That was the tragedy of the union between East and West at Florence. The leaders united without the people – and there could be no permanence in that.

If we may be bold in the hope of our faith – and why not, when the Bible speaks of faith that moves mountains? – then on their meeting – no doubt not easily achieved – we can imagine "Peter, Paul, and John" saluting one another with the kiss of peace and laying hands upon one another in their own names and as representatives of all the servants of the church who stand behind them. They would thus add to what for many separated brethren hitherto had been objectively at least uncertain, and what as the sign of pastoral authority for "the part of the flock entrusted to your charge" can always be given where belief in the Lord, devotion to his service, and love of unity exist. It is true that the ordained will be unable to allow themselves to be re-ordained; but as imposition of hands is at the same time a sign of forgiving love, of the desire for peace, of the blessing of Christ, therefore, from the "manifold grace" of all would come to each, that grace to which he was receptive. Suddenly much would change, men would face each other as brothers. The particular traditions which the confessions have evolved in their separation – sometimes in opposition to each other, sometimes without thinking at all of each other – these things could be left to be compared in common consultation, and judged against the one rule of revelation, the *ultimum fundamentum* of all the church's thought and action. Or would Peter II dig in his heels and say "I"? But the others would do well to ask themselves, for Christ's sake, if "for the sake of love's understanding"[372] they are not being exhorted to turn themselves towards the one centre; because Jesus desired unity – even that made visible in Peter.

It is the hope born of the Christian faith, and not any prophecy, which tells us that "Peter, Paul, and John" will be able to take up the thread of conversation again at the place where once the rift occurred. It occurred, not because the Church wanted it, but at the will of politicians. At that time neither the theologians of the *Confessio Augustana* nor the fathers of the Council of Trent were able, as they would have liked[373], to convene as an ecumenical council in which all had a part. They hoped that this might be accomplished in the future, and this for ever remains the hope of the Christian world.

[372] Council of Chalcedon.
[373] L. v. Pastor: *Paul III* (1909) 31 ff.